"In this lovely and loving memoir, *Junior Bonner: The Making of a Classic with Steven McQueen and Sam Peckinpah in the Summer of 1971*, Jeb Rosebrook recalls the production of the film from its beginnings in his own masterly screenplay—an original and one of the best Peckinpah was ever graced with—to the disappointing returns that greeted the film at the box office. Yet, like the story in front of the camera, the story Rosebrook finds behind the camera is not one of defeat but of faith in dreams and perseverance in pursuing them—it's a story of creative *collaboration*, where every-one working to his or her peak capacity contributes to the final achievement."

—Paul Seydor, author of *Peckinpah: The Western Films: A Recon-sideration* and *The Authentic Death and Contentious Afterlife of Pat Garrett* and *Billy the Kid: The Untold Story of Peckinpah's Last Western Film*.

Junior Bonner

The Making of a Classic with Steve McQueen and Sam Peckinpah in the Summer of 1971

Steve McQueen embraced his title role as the aging rodeo star in Junior Bonner.

Rosebrook Family Collection.

Junior Bonner

The Making of a Classic with Steve McQueen and Sam Peckinpah in the Summer of 1971

By Jeb Rosebrook

with Stuart Rosebrook

Foreword by Marshall Terrill

Junior Bonner: The Making of a Classic with Steve McQueen and Sam Peckinpah in the Summer of 1971
By Jeb Rosebrook with Stuart Rosebrook. Foreword by Marshall Terrill

North American Rights
© 2018 Jeb Rosebrook
Quo Vadis Communications LLC
P.O. Box 1267
Scottsdale, AZ 85252

Published in the USA by:
BearManor Media
P O Box 71426
Albany, Georgia 31708
www.bearmanormedia.com

ISBN: 978-1-62933-290-1
BearManor Media, Albany, Georgia
Printed in the United States of America
Book Text Design: Robbie Adkins, www.adkinsconsult.com

Front Cover Captions:

Steve McQueen believed Junior Bonner *and the title role was one of his career's best.* Jeff Slater Collection.

Junior Bonner *screenwriter Jeb Rosebrook was not only on set in Prescott all summer in 1971, he also earned an honorary membership in the stuntman's association for participating in the wild cow-milking event in Prescott's Frontier Days Rodeo and the fight scene in the Palace Bar.* Rosebrook Family Collection.

On location in Prescott, Arizona, in the summer of 1971, director Sam Peckinpah worked closely with his star Steve McQueen and screenwriter Jeb Rosebrook to make Junior Bonner, *what he and many others, including McQueen, considered one of the finest movies of his career.* Jeff Slater Collection.

Also by Jeb Rosebrook

Forever More
Purgatory Road
Saturday

Junior Bonner *horizontal one sheet, ABC Pictures, 1972.*
Mike Siegel Collection.

Dedication

This memoir is dedicated to my wife, Dorothy, of fifty-seven years, and to our two lovingly loyal children, Stuart and Katherine.

To the late Eunice Fischer, who never lost faith.

And to friends and mentors, Max Evans and the late Earl Hamner.

And to those who brought Junior to life: Steve and Sam, Joe Wizan, Martin Baum and Mike Wise.

To the people of Prescott, Arizona, and the memorable summer of 1971.

To the Orme Family and those I grew up with in Yavapai County, most especially Uncle Chick and Aunt Minna, Charlie and Mimi, Mort and Lynn, Katie and Bruce McDonald, and the McDonald Family of Mayer.

Finally, to all the sons who wrote me saying how much the film meant to their relationship with their father.

TABLE OF CONTENTS

Acknowledgments

There are many who pointed me to the trail that this memoir follows—Keith Woods, Marshall Terrill, and my son, Stuart—who, for the past several years have urged me to record the journey from page one to the filming of *Junior Bonner* in Prescott, Arizona, in the summer of 1971.

R. Kirk (Sandy) Dunbar, who literally, in July 1970, put me on the road to meeting Junior and his family.

Earl Hamner, Jr., who found the office in his writing building in Studio City, California, where, on January 1, 1968, I set out to become a writer.

Max Evans, who came into the lives of the Rosebrook family because of Sam Peckinpah's trial with the Writers Guild of America in 1973.

The late Mike Wise of Creative Artists Agency, into whose agent's life I entered after my fortunes met failures that taught me lessons to endure.

The late producer Joe Wizan who optioned a four-page outline called *Bonner*, and then my pages for the screenplay *Junior Bonner*, which in the end put us together in Prescott in the summer of 1971.

What followed was the collaboration with Steve McQueen and Sam Peckinpah and the day-to-day journey in the making of *Junior Bonner*.

And I am forever grateful to William "Bill" Pierce, location manager on *Junior Bonner*. Without Bill, Prescott's representative on the Arizona Film Commission, and the Prescott Jaycees Rodeo Chairman for the 84th Annual Prescott Frontier Days Rodeo and Parade, the film would never have been made in Prescott. Bill's ability to work with Sam Peckinpah and Joe Wizan sealed the deal in those tension-filled days when we were all waiting for the green-light to be given for production in Prescott.

To the poet laureate Jim Ciletti, who I met, young writers both, at the inaugural Orme School Fine Arts Festival in 1969, for reminding the boy who left home at age nine that so many of his written characters were trying to get home. To those who came on early and stayed late: Paul Mielche Mielche, who took my first original screenplay, *Ward Craft*, and shaped what might have been a James Coburn classic, but what was not to be. Producer Norman Rosemont and director Fielder Cook, who quickly became a close friend of the family, took me back to my boyhood home in New York on *Miracle on 34th Street* (CBS, 1973), as did Phil Capice and Harvey Hart on *Prince of Central Park* (CBS, 1977). And, for the chance from Ted Strauss and Stan Margolis of the Wolper Company, who gambled on me to write the true story of *Chief Joseph, I Will Fight No More Forever* (ABC, 1976).

To Casey Tibbs, whose road home from the rodeo and Hollywood always led to ours in North Hollywood and an important friendship with our family.

Joe Byrne, my partner, who preached "story," blending drama and humor into our collaborative work.

John Wilder, whose writing and producing accomplishments rank him among the greatest in the television medium—for teaching the lesson of dramatic dialogue.

And agents Tony Ludwig, Bill Haber, Elliot Webb, Mark Pariser, Mickey Freiberg, and agent/manager Elizabeth Robinson.

I would also like to thank Barbara Leigh for her insightful chapters on Steve and Sam, and the film company, in her autobiography with Marshall Terrill.

To Katy Haber, whose friendship began in the summer of 1971, and continues through today.

To the generosity of Peckinpah's historians and critics, Marshall Terrill, Mike Siegel, Jeff Slater, Paul Seydor, Steve Gaydos, and I am grateful for the fateful meeting on the WGA strike line with Garner Simmons. This book would not be the same if it was not for Mike Siegel and Jeff Slater sharing images from their personal Peckinpah collections.

To the thoughtful team who contributed their help, insights, and contacts on our search for the history behind the music of Rod Hart, Alex Taylor, and Jerry Fielding in *Junior Bonner*: Jim West; Mike Siegel; Todd Roberts; Michael Blake; fraternity brother, singer-songwriter Mark Allen; David MacKechnie; BMI/ASCAP in New York and Los Angeles; Songs of Universal, Inc.; Al Gomes of Big Noise Now; Eileen McNulty and Howard Green at Disney Studios; Jon Burlingame, music and soundtrack historian; Margaret Herrick Library, Academy of Motion Picture Arts & Sciences, Beverly Hills, California; and, the L. Tom Perry Special Collections, BYU Library, Ogden, Utah.

To Merle Frost, Darlene, and his family, for their support during the leanest of years.

To Tim Young, screenwriter and private eye, who's always been available to me for "location" work!

To the late Don Congdon and Jack Foster.

To the late Dr. George Foster of Washington and Lee University who, after reading a series of my first short stories said, "You are a sophomore. In Greek, sophomore means 'wise fool.' Keep writing."

To John and Jean Rosebrook, who gave me up at age nine to the Orme Family of Mayer, Arizona, and their Quarter Circle V Bar Ranch School in 1945.

And to Father Rafael and Father Bede of St. Leo's Prep, who fostered a discipline of writing and love of reading.

For all who read the manuscript and assisted us in the editing— Beth Deveny, Marshall Terrill, Jim Ciletti, John Farkis, and my son Stuart.

To the great support of family, who have supported and encouraged me from the start: my daughter Katherine R. Goode, her husband, Robert, and grandchildren Fallon Goode and Jack Goode, and Stuart, his wife, Julie E. Rosebrook, and grandchildren Jeb Rosebrook and Kristina Rosebrook.

Finally, to my faithful archivist, constructive critic, and always my supporter, Dorothy, my incredible wife, who has gone down the road of a writer's life with me for fifty-seven years.

FOREWORD

Writers share a unique and friendly bond. Perhaps it's because we intimately know each other's war stories—the amount of work it takes to see the printed word transformed into book form; the sacrifices families and loved ones make for the author; why a book "advance" is really code for "token amount," and "royalties" are for people like J.K. Rowling, James Patterson, Patricia Cornwell, and John Grisham.

I instantly bonded with Jeb Rosebrook the moment we first spoke for my 1993 biography *Steve McQueen: Portrait of an American Rebel*. In fact, we share many bonds—as writers, Phoenicians, lovers of Arizona history and culture, and boxing fans.

The real cement, though, has always been Steve McQueen. I've written about McQueen extensively in six books thus far; Jeb wrote a film for the legendary star, which showcased his true abilities as an actor and has developed a worldwide cult following over the years. In other words, my knowledge is secondhand; Jeb's is straight from the horse's mouth.

Jeb was one of the first people I interviewed for my debut biography, and that puts me forever in his debt. I was a rookie writer doing a book on speculation and Jeb was gracious enough to grant me a very long and engaging interview regarding his experiences on *Junior Bonner*. At the time Jeb was residing in California while I was living across the country in Washington, D.C. A few years later we both moved to the Phoenix area, and have enjoyed a true friendship ever since, which extends to his lovely wife, Dorothy, and son, Stuart.

At the time, I doubt this book that you now hold in your hands was ever contemplated by Jeb. Over the years Stuart and I started tag-teaming Jeb, gently nagging him to write an account of the making of the rodeo film starring Steve McQueen and helmed by maverick director Sam Peckinpah. He did an abridged piece for *Arizona Highways* magazine in 2001, but that was the G-rated version.

Over the years, Jeb told me stories about *Junior Bonner* that he probably had planned to take to the grave because of his cowboy code. He didn't believe in gossip—at least the printed kind. His stories left you salivating, and always wanting more. I don't know if we convinced Jeb or not, but I was thrilled beyond belief when he told me about a year ago he was finally going to write this book.

It's important that Jeb chronicles the alpha and omega of this important motion picture because Jeb was the only screenwriter from start to finish on *Junior Bonner*, with his name listed on the final credits. Jeb was on the set of the movie throughout the ten-week shoot in the summer of '71, and watched his vision unfold with a superstar actor, superstar director, and an unforgettable ensemble cast.

It's also important to note that Steve McQueen rarely gave interviews, and when he did, he didn't talk much about his craft or film work. When pressed, however, he usually cited *The Thomas Crown Affair* (1968) and *Junior Bonner* (1972) as his favorite film performances. The latter came on the heels of a high-profile failure, the ill-fated *Le Mans* (1971). McQueen had been a major movie star for almost a decade and had experienced the "Star Trip" of booze, drugs, indiscriminate sex, and wasn't always so nice in his climb to the top. For years McQueen had been sticking it to producers and studios, and he was due for a karmic kickback.

Le Mans took away all of his box-office heat, and was a reminder that he wasn't omnipotent and all-powerful. In one fell swoop, he lost his wife, agent, production company, and his personal fortune, thanks to the Internal Revenue Service, who presented him with a $2 million bill for back taxes.

His comeback was in direct contrast to *Le Mans*; for his next film, he wanted a "quiet picture" and a character-oriented role in which he wasn't required to do all of the dramatic lifting. The decision paid off handsomely for McQueen, who turned in one of the most poignant and wistful performances of his career in *Junior Bonner*.

McQueen loved how the script tapped into the symbiotic relationship between the passing of the old and new West. He nicknamed Jeb

The on-screen chemistry between Steve McQueen and Barbara Leigh in their respective roles as Junior Bonner and Charmagne was easy to create because they were also dating during the production of Junior Bonner *in the summer of 1971. McQueen biographer Marshall Terrill is also co-author of Leigh's autobiography* The King, McQueen and the Love Machine: My Secret Hollywood Life with Elvis Presley, Steve McQueen and the Smiling Cobra. Rosebrook Family Collection.

"Shakespeare" because of his gift for dialogue, and signed with ABC Pictures Corp., in April 1971 to make *Junior Bonner* his next picture. This memoir surprised me because it contains many gems: like the time actress Susan Hayward was taken to an extravagant dinner and romanced for a large role. But somehow in the fog of alcohol and ego, no one actually thought to formally extend her an offer, which she was ready to take after a long hiatus from film. The part eventually went to Ida Lupino, who was brilliant. Or how Peckinpah tried many times to put his name on the script and have Jeb fired from his own movie. And how Jeb, a struggling screenwriter, ended up buying McQueen (the highest-paid movie star of his era) a beer on the last day of production because the superstar didn't carry cash on him.

But I don't want to give away too many of his secrets. Let Jeb's brilliant and vivid memory take you back to the cowboy town of Prescott, Arizona, during the early 1970s, and the making of a modern-day classic that Steve McQueen predicted would find its audience in time.

Now is that time.

—Marshall Terrill, author of:
Steve McQueen: Portrait of an American Rebel
Steve McQueen: The Last Mile
Steve McQueen: A Tribute to the King of Cool
Steve McQueen: The Life and Legend of a Hollywood Icon
Steve McQueen: Le Mans in the Rearview Mirror
Steve McQueen: The Salvation of an American Icon

"Why am I called Junior?"
—*Steve McQueen*

"This was Jeb Rosebrook, who lived and worked rodeo and got the script to Steve McQueen. That was Jeb Rosebrook—a damn fine writer."
—*Sam Peckinpah*

Junior Bonner (1972) is the best rodeo film that's ever been made. It was the best script Sam ever got his hands on.
–*Max Evans author of* Goin' Crazy with Sam Peckinpah and All Our Friends as told to Robert Nott

"A cowboy never leaves his hat on the bed."
—*Ben Johnson*

"That's a goddamn poem."
—*Warren Oates, at the debut screening of* Junior Bonner *at Grauman's Chinese Theater, 1972*

"An elevator operator in New York makes more money than you do."
—*John B. Rosebrook*

PROLOGUE

The writer arrived at Warner Brothers on a cool early November afternoon.

He met the producer, whose name was Joe Wizan. He was the writer's age, thirty-five. As it turned out, an Aquarius and a Gemini.

He had read the writer's three-and-a-half-page outline. He offered to option it, giving the writer enough money to create a screenplay from the outline. The writer, soon to be on the doorstep of no money at all, eagerly accepted.

Joe Wizan told the writer he wanted the screenplay for the highest paid actor in the world: Steve McQueen.

The writer was me, Jeb Rosebrook.

Sam Peckinpah's opening montage and credit sequence of Junior Bonner *included a black-and-white sequence of* Steve McQueen's *character being injured in a bull ride with his nemesis, a notorious bull named Sunshine.*
Jeff Slater Collection.

ACT ONE

The boy often watched the seasons from the window of his Connecticut bedroom. From there he saw the green of summer; the winds of autumn sending leaves tumbling; the snow of winter, bright against birch trees; and the promise of spring, the once-again leafing of trees.

The boy loved his Eden Avenue home just outside of Springdale. There were the Price brothers up the street—Beans and George—and Mr. Thompson down the road, who lived alone in a small house and was suspected, with his large overseas radio, of being a German spy. And Joan Halloran further down Eden, three years older, and as close as a big sister could be to him.

The boy loved the small brook running through his backyard. He loved the stone wall dividing his homeland from the woods behind the wall. He would travel alone through the woods to Joan's house, crossing the rocks over brooks, over the flourishing skunk cabbage, returning to Eden Avenue, where teenagers and servicemen parked in seclusion and littered the ground with what older boys would tell him were called "rubbers."

He loved Willard School at Turn of River, Connecticut, especially a girl named Lois and his friend, Dennis Mulrooney, who joined him in afternoon Catechism classes at Saint Cecelia's Catholic Church in Springdale. He found escape in a growing collection of comic books—especially superheroes Superman, Captain Marvel, and Batman, as well as Classics Illustrated Comics' *The Count of Monte Cristo* and *The Three Musketeers*, and inquiring into the teenage mind with *Archie and Veronica*.

He loved movies, too. He often went with his mother to theaters in Stamford to see films starring actors like Gary Cooper and Alan Ladd. With his friends, he loved the cowboy movies, especially with Gene Autry and William "Wild Bill" Elliott as Red Ryder.

And, of course, the *Gene Autry* and *Red Ryder* comic books and *Hopalong Cassidy*, too!

The boy's life was enriched by his father, John ("Jack") Rosebrook, a high-profile, successful copywriter for Madison Avenue's Young & Rubicam advertising agency, and by his mother, Jean, once a show girl who danced in *George White's Scandals of 1924* and *1925*.

Both had lost their fathers when they were very young. John's father, Charles, a college graduate, sorted mail on the rail line between Detroit and his home in Cincinnati—a job he held because he could read. He caught the influenza plague sorting mail and died in 1901. John was four. His mother, Frances, borrowed $500 from her father to build a rooming house for co-eds at her alma mater, Ohio Wesleyan University in Delaware, Ohio. This way she put her four children, John the third youngest, through college.

Jean's father, Francis Xavier Fallon, a Tammany Hall-appointed sewer inspector and sometime seller of imported sponges from Cuba in the Bronx, father of six girls and husband to Mary, died of uremic poisoning. Jean was six in 1909 when her father died. Mary took in sewing. The oldest, Cecelia and Florence, grades eight and six, went to work.

A lover of Civil War history, John purchased 298 acres in Carter's Bridge, Virginia, outside of Charlottesville in 1940. The house was re-built, and a mill operating on the Hardware River became a Jean and John enterprise to sell cornmeal by mail, while John planted ten acres of native American grapes, for what was to be the largest vineyard in Virginia, and raised Black Angus cattle. In honor of their marriage seven years earlier at the Ambassador Hotel in Manhattan, the newly owned land was called "Falrose Farm." (The farm's name was derived from my mother's maiden name, Fallon and Rosebrook, thus Falrose, which later became the name of my corporation.)

Life for the boy was thus divided between Connecticut, Virginia, and visits to Manhattan, where his mother had reunion lunches with former *Scandals* cast members, as well as lunch with his parents. The boy met World War II from a train window passing the New York docks where the sabotaged French liner *Normandy* lay capsized on its side.

Summer began with the red clay land of Virginia. He became part of the families of tenant farmers who worked for John and Jean. He went barefoot. He wore bib overalls. He learned to drive a team of horses named George and Nell.

Yet, from the age of two, the boy was often not well. The boy had what was termed by his doctor, allergy asthma. Because of it he was allergic to his Labrador dog, Jackson; his feather pillows; his bedroom rug; humidity; and cold weather. He wheezed and he coughed and had difficulty breathing, and he missed more school than he wanted. He was often in bed. Each week, at age eight, in hopes of relieving his condition, he received a shot in either arm.

And it was equally bad in Virginia with the morning ground fog sweeping across the land, causing him to wheeze in attempts to keep his breath.

In the autumn of 1944, the boy's ninth year, the Connecticut doctor advised his father and mother that he should go away to a climate that would help him regain his health.

In February 1945, the boy, accompanied by his mother, boarded a train in Grand Central Station in New York City, leaving his home on Eden Avenue, bound for a new life at a school on a working cattle ranch, the Quarter Circle V Bar Ranch School in central Arizona.

The boy was me.

I would never be home with my parents again for more than three months out of the year.

1970

I was now thirty-five. Except for a year and a half in the ninth and tenth grades with the Benedictines at Saint Leo Prep in Dade City, Florida, I had spent my life—as a student, ranch hand, and summer camp counselor with the Orme Family—as a part of a land I came to know as if my own. The 27,000-acre Quarter Circle V Bar Ranch was located in Yavapai County, near the town of Mayer, approximately thirty miles from the county seat of Prescott, and ninety miles north of Phoenix—all by dirt road.

In early July, while with my wife, Dorothy, and our children, Jeb Stuart, seven, and Katherine Fallon, four, visiting Dorothy's widowed mother, Eunice, in Phoenix, a friend of those Orme days, R. Kirk "Sandy" Dunbar, invited me to join him in attending the July Frontier Days Rodeo, billed as the "World's Oldest Rodeo" in Prescott, Arizona.

Eagerly, I accepted his invitation.

I believed the land I knew and loved was awaiting my return. The land of Yavapai County, where Ash Creek ran between the mesas, where cottonwoods shared the land with sycamore and black walnut trees. A land spread with mesquite and, by the law of nature, the mesquite did not green until there was no danger of frost. It was this land that I knew, where white-faced cattle grazed and where in spring and fall, I had ridden in many roundups.

Years had passed. This was my homecoming. Or escaping truth, real life?

Dorothy and I had been married going on ten years. When we met, she was a beautiful young woman of nineteen, having finished her sophomore year at the University of Arizona in Tucson. I was a recent Manhattan transplant, employed as the assistant advertising manager of Diamond's Department Store in Phoenix's Park Central shopping center. Her summer job was in sportswear. In time we would date exclusively. As a graduate of Washington and Lee University in Lexington, Virginia, all male, with only all-female schools to date, I discovered the Delta Gamma sorority at the University of Arizona—a brand new world of pulchritude! We were married August 6, 1960.

Now thirty-five years old and living in the North Hollywood area of Los Angeles, I was an ex-advertising executive with Foote, Cone & Belding, and, with *Saturday* (E.P. Dutton, 1965), a published novelist. Venturing out on my own in 1968 to become a full-time writer, I rented an office downstairs from my friend and mentor from my paid internship at NBC in New York in the summer of 1956, Earl Hamner, Jr., in Studio City, just a few miles from our home.

Earl had followed his own path to a writing career in Los Angeles in 1961, just after publication of his second novel, *Spencer's Mountain* (1963), and its subsequent purchase and filming by Warner

Brothers in 1962. Earl had left his writing job with NBC Radio in New York and, after some struggles and a fortuitous reintroduction to his post-World War II University of Cincinnati classmate Rod Serling, sold two spec scripts to Serling's *Twilight Zone* (CBS, 1959–1964). He quickly became one of Serling's go-to writers.

Through Earl's recommendation I secured a writing assignment at Universal Studios on *The Virginian* (NBC, 1962–1971) television series. My only episode, "The Bugler," aired July 18, 1969, although Dorothy and I did not see it until 2013 on the Westerns Channel because the West Coast feed was preempted by national television coverage of Apollo 11's moon approach. I received story credit and shared the teleplay credit with Gerry Day, a pioneer of women writers in Hollywood who was brought into my first production by producer Howard Christie. Universal then offered me a standard exclusive seven-year contract. I would, however, be paid only if I sold a story idea to one of the studio's contract producers and they, in turn, sold it to one of the networks. With no guarantee of a regular paycheck, I turned down the offer.

What to do? One choice only: write an original screenplay. With Earl's help in shaping the story, I adapted a character from my novel *Saturday* into a contemporary Western. My literary agent at Creative Management Associates, Mike Wise, got the script, titled *Ward Craft*, optioned by actor James Coburn, who was starring on location in Louisiana in the production of the Tennessee Williams and Gore Vidal screenplay, *The Last of the Mobile Hotshots* (1970). Coburn's manager and close confidant, Jim Logan, a seemingly brilliant man of hippiedom, chose my screenplay because he envisioned the project could become for Coburn what *Five Easy Pieces* (1970) was for Jack Nicholson. *Ward Craft* was the story of a World War II paratrooper, an Arizona cowboy whose claim to fame was a Silver Star awarded for bravery in Europe, who was now forgotten as his hometown gathered to honor a Vietnam paratrooper hero, a Native American.

There were problems.

Two major ones. Emotional and financial.

I had failed, despite a generous advance from Dutton, to publish my second novel, *Copper Station*. Because *Saturday* was so well received by Dutton and critics, the publisher invited me to write a second novel for them. I did an outline and submitted three chapters. It was a novel of post-war Arizona. I simply got lost in my own story. My editor, Peggy Brooks, tried to help but we just could not pull it together. This was 1966-'67 and I was still working for Foote, Cone & Belding advertising, and writing at night. When I left the agency on January 1, 1968, to try to write for a living, I followed the advice of the famous sci-fi writer Ray Bradbury and wrote a short ten-page story every week and had it in the mail by Friday. I did this for five months or so and sold one story to *Cavalier* magazine. I still had the unpublished novel on my desk and tried revising *Copper Station*, despite my New York literary agent having set me up with representation at Adams, Ray and Rosenberg (Earl Hamner's agency) in Hollywood.

Nothing worked, and then Earl ran into Howard Christie, a producer at Universal. Earl had written "The Wanda Snow Story" episode of *Wagon Train* (1965) for Howard. Earl was busy on another series and recommended untried me. By that time the hot agency had given up on me and another agency was paying little attention to me. Howard called me in and put me to work on *The Virginian* (1961–1971), which he was then producing, resulting in the aforementioned production of "The Bugler."

My success with *The Virginian* led to an early lesson in the writers' world of Hollywood.

I had written a story concept titled "Keeper," about Indians and Appalachians living in the same neighborhood in Chicago. My agent sent it to producer Walter Mirisch, who had just received the Oscar for Best Picture for *In the Heat of the Night* (1967). He hired me to work with Mark Rydell, who had just formed his own company with Sidney Pollack, and completed the production of *The Reivers* (1969) starring Steve McQueen.

They sent me off with photographer Don Dornan to the coal mines of West Virginia and the conflicted Indian/Appalachian area of Chicago, but Rydell had me take my simple story of an Appalachian deaf mute and an Indian girl into a Vietnam war story, and I got canned off my own story. I have seen Mark at social occasions in the years since and I always remind him "you're the man who fired me off my own story," and we laugh.

By then, during my time on *Keeper*, I had moved to new representation at Creative Management Associates (CMA) and top first-assistant director Bob Westman at Universal had read *Saturday*. He wanted to turn *Ward Craft* into a contemporary Western. I said I hoped he would option it, as I was broke. He said he talked it over with his wife and she wanted to save money for a house. I had coffee with Earl every afternoon. I told him and he suggested much of a plot. I did it on my own, finishing in May of 1970, and gave it to my new agent, Mike Wise, at CMA. In June, fellow CMA client James Coburn, who had just finished his fourteenth feature film since costarring with James Garner and Julie Andrews in *The Americanization of Emily* (1964), optioned *Ward Craft*. This got the Rosebrooks some money in the bank and, importantly, inside the doors of the most successful talent agencies in town with one of its top actors.

A month later, my life changed. I went to the rodeo in Prescott and Junior was born—four years after the death of *Copper Station* and my failed journey with Walter Mirisch and Mark Rydell.

The second (due to the first) and more serious problem was my marriage. Dorothy, while proud of a published novelist and produced television writer, desperately missed the security of being the wife of a steady wage-earning advertising executive.

After I received the advance on *Ward Craft*, Dorothy and I decided to take a much-needed family vacation to Phoenix, Arizona, in late June of 1970. We stayed with Dorothy's mom, Eunice Fischer. Phoenix was time out of time; to take a deep breath in one relatively secure moment, and think hard about what comes next after Jim Coburn. How long would Jim Coburn's $1,800 option last before the Rosebrook family was again searching for true financial security? When would *Ward Craft* be produced?

There damn well better be something.

We had been in Phoenix a few days when my good friend, R. Kirk Dunbar, invited me to go to Prescott for the Frontier Days Rodeo. I realized it had been fifteen years since I had attended the "World's Oldest Rodeo."

A day at the rodeo was an escape. It was a return to a world I had known: cowboys, rodeo competition (in my debut in the Phoenix 20-30 Club World Championship Junior Rodeo, I failed as a header in the team roping), cowboy bars, and Country-Western music. It was a time when the jukebox played Webb Pierce and "There Stands the Glass" (w. Mary Jean Shurtz, Russ Hull, and Audrey Grisham) as you honky-tonked the night away in Flagstaff's Museum Club. The music slowed and there was a young woman in your arms and Eddy Arnold sang about how many lips had kissed her, but "I Really Don't Want to Know" (w. Don Robertson-Howard Barns).

For that afternoon, I was transported back into those days of the past as I shared the grandstands with those who had been of my own kind, relishing the arena moments of bronc riders and bull riders, of those who chased wild cows with a milk bottle, of the timing competition of young women and their horses rounding the barrels and speeding for the finish line, and the clowns, brave bull fighters, and otherwise, endlessly pursuing audience laughter.

After the rodeo, we were transported back into the smoke and drink and dancing on Prescott's Whiskey Row.

Yet the pressures of marriage and money remained tight around me. It showed when a young woman and her cowboy danced past me. Our eyes met. She had but one word for me as she danced by, "Smile."

Am I trapped by my own idealism? I wondered.

***

Fourteen years earlier, in 1956 between my junior and senior years at Washington and Lee University, my dad, head of the Copy Department at Young & Rubicam Advertising on New York's Madison Avenue, had arranged an interview for me for a paid internship as a television writer for NBC.

Shortly after my 21st birthday in June, I reported for work at NBC. I was supervised by network executive Ross Donaldson, who reported on my progress to a talent programmer, a former Hollywood agent, Nat Wolfe, who, in turn, reported to NBC president Pat Weaver.

Donaldson had me work on two original teleplays. He would read my progress on one while I worked on the second one. For guidance on story and structure, he had me reading writers Paddy Chayefsky, Rod Serling, and other contemporaries of television's Golden Age.

In this summer of 1956, I met Earl Hamner, twelve years my senior. Because of my summers at Falrose Farm at Carter's Bridge, Virginia, I had become a sometime dirt road, red clay child. Earl was from the neighboring rural town of Schuyler in nearby Nelson County.

We met at NBC. "My cousin works there," Earl's cousin, Charles, told me one afternoon when he and my Carter's Bridge friend Peter Hjorth had stopped to visit me at Washington and Lee. Charles was a senior at Virginia Tech University in Blacksburg. Charles' dad owned the store in Schuyler while Earl's father worked in the stone quarry. "What's he do at NBC?" I asked. "He writes books," Charles replied. (Charles would become Dr. Charles Hamner, heading up the University of Virginia Medical Center before becoming president of the North Carolina Biotechnical Institute and known throughout the scientific world for his work in biochemistry.)

I had my job interview but no time to ask about Charles' cousin. While changing planes in Washington, I looked over the paperback book selection and saw Fifty Roads to Town, *a novel by Earl Hamner, Jr. Indeed, he did write books! And no less published by Random House!*

When we met that summer day, Earl was working on a radio series titled Biography in Sound. *He has just completed a show on the life of author* Thomas Wolfe. *("Well, Tom was born..." began an aunt.)*

Earl, then thirty-three, became my friend and mentor from that day on, until his passing at age ninety-two, on March 24, 2016.

***

After the rodeo, as Dunbar drove me back to my family in Phoenix, I looked upon the land I had known—the land I believed had been awaiting my return.

Rangeland had disappeared. There was a sign announcing "The Town of Prescott Valley." There were newly built homes for sale. Where cattle had once grazed, there were now homes.

Hell, Rosebrook, what did you expect? You knew a dirt road to Prescott. Why shouldn't it be paved now? This was 1970. Where there is pavement, there must be traffic lights. Sure, and a strip mall, even a motel inviting visitors.

Hell, Rosebrook, times changed. You forgot to change with them.
The Town of Prescott Valley, Established 1966. Population 1,400.
Hey, Rosebrook, where have you been?
We returned to Phoenix and enjoyed time with family and friends. Stuart spent time at the Orme Summer Camp, and in my quiet time at Eunice's with Dorothy and Katherine, I was able to begin the thought process on a screenplay based on a rodeo rider and a change in the landscape I had just discovered. The summer of 1970 was one to remember for all of us—except I did not have an outline of my new screenplay and because of the need for money, I was writing by the seat of my pants.

During Labor Day weekend, our phone in North Hollywood rang. Mike Wise had a question. "Robert Redford wants a rodeo story. Do you have one?"

Since returning from the Prescott rodeo, no one knew I had been trying to write a rodeo screenplay. Inspired by my experience, yes, but plunging into the script without an outline, I was going nowhere. Was this to be *Keeper* all over again? With only me to blame?

Robert Redford. A rodeo story. Did I have one?

It's hard to explain what happened that weekend. If you believe prayers are sometimes answered, I sat in front of my typewriter, my dad's 1948 Royal portable, and wrote three and a half pages of a story outline called *Bonner*, the story of a rodeo rider returning to his hometown of Prescott, reuniting with his mother, seeing his younger brother changing the landscape with homes and retirement living schemes, and having the challenge to ride a bull named Sunshine.

Yes, Robert Redford needs a rodeo story and now he has one.

The dreams that soared that Labor Day weekend fell into six weeks of silence. No word from Robert Redford. Nothing from Jim Coburn or his manager Jim Logan. CMA had given no indication that *Ward Craft* would be produced any time soon. The option money was heading toward zero.

October was on its journey to November. Was this to be the end of my journey? (My last rodeo!)

It was not an easy call to make. "Mike, I'm tapped out."

Mike replied, "I'll get back to you."

Would he?

Two days later, he did. "I have an appointment for you to meet a producer named Joe Wizan at Warner Brothers. Tomorrow afternoon." And so it was. Joe was a tall, lean, well-tanned man of my age, thirty-five. His easy smile masked intensity. He always appeared confident and relaxed, in that order. (After all, I would later learn, this was a young man who earned his way through UCLA by playing poker.)

Joe had climbed the Hollywood ladder, first as a driver for a major agent at the William Morris Agency, then to Creative Management Agency as an agent. He was mentored by uber agent Martin Baum, until he made his move, having become well-acquainted with CMA's major stars, writers, and directors, to become a motion picture producer.

Joe had paid aspiring screenwriter and director John Milius $5,000 for a screenplay based on the life of legendary mountain man John "Liver Eating" Johnson. His Warner Brothers office was involved in pre-production for the film prior to going to Utah for filming with director Sidney Pollack. Eventually the film would be retitled *Jeremiah Johnson* (1972). The star was a CMA client, Robert Redford.

A word of backstory on Joe: His Jewish parents had fled Europe and gone to Mexico and from there emigrated to the United States and Los Angeles. Joe's father opened a furniture store in East Los Angeles, which might as well have been Mexico. Joe and his best friend, also Jewish, Mickey Borofsky, went to Roosevelt High School. Life was hardly easy for one of the few White-Jewish kids in racially tense East L.A. When Joe and his friend Mickey went to see *Shane* (1953), Joe's dreams of Hollywood were born. Unbeknownst to him at the time, his high school days at Roosevelt High prepared him well for the competition of the Hollywood system. When not in school, he was learning sales at his parents' furniture store.

It did not take long for the poker player to place his chips on me. Joe had received investment money for future projects from a Washington State heir to a lumber fortune, Booth Gardner, and a Seattle advertising executive, and he wished to use a portion of that money on *Bonner*. Option money in the amount of $1,800, which would provide me time to write the screenplay.

Joe then added, "I want this for Steve McQueen."

I went home with his handshake.

Steve McQueen? Dorothy looked at me. Sure, nice talk. Hollywood talk.

Within a day, I had my check—$1,800 against $50,000 if the picture was made.

The next week Mike sent me the contract. Joe Wizan Productions. I snatched up the closest pen and I signed.

Steve McQueen? Like millions of others, I knew him well from the movies. He was a rough cut Paul Newman. He was a kick in *The Blob* (1958), then onward and upward for me in *The Magnificent Seven* (1960) with Coburn, *The War Lover* (1962) (I had read the novel), *The Great Escape* (1963), *Love with the Proper Stranger* (1963), *The Cincinnati Kid* (1965), *Nevada Smith* (1966) (also read the novel), *The Sand Pebbles* (1966) (*loved* the novel), *The Thomas Crown Affair* (1968), *Bullitt* (1968), and *The Reivers* (1969). I had heard via newspaper gossip that he wanted the part of Rocky Graziano in *Somebody Up There Likes Me* (1956) because he was personally more like Rocky than the well-heeled and college-educated Paul Newman. I also read that his most recent effort, *Le Mans* (1971), was a creative and troubled picture, possibly heading for disaster.

It would be the end of December before Joe headed for Utah to produce *Jeremiah Johnson*.

He wasted little time with our working schedule.

Research: Caroll Ballard's brilliant documentary, *Rodeo* (1969), on the 1968 National Finals Rodeo in Oklahoma City made memorable with a longtime bull rider named Warren Granger "Freckles" Brown riding Tornado, a bull who had never been ridden. Owned by rodeo great Jim Shoulders, Tornado had thrown two hundred riders in fourteen years, but Freckles, forty-six years old, stayed the eight seconds.

Lesson learned: Junior Bonner returning to his hometown of Prescott to ride a bull named Sunshine. A bull that had never been ridden.

Research: Dorothy and I joining Joe at the Los Angeles Forum for a World Championship Rodeo.

Routine: Jeb will write ten-to-fifteen pages and send them to Utah. Joe will read and make suggestions and possible changes. While Joe is doing this, Jeb will continue on. Brick by brick, a script will be written, keeping in mind the July 4th rodeo in Prescott.

For Christmas in Phoenix, where this journey had begun, with Dorothy, Stuart, Katherine, and Dorothy's mother, Eunice, my Royal portable traveled with us.

Into my mind came a first name for Bonner—Junior.

And where in the original outline, Junior had a mother named Elvira, he now had a father named very simply, "Ace." And Ace has a dog named Dougal. Ace and Elvira are separated. Junior has a younger brother named Curly. He is building Sunrise Estates for seniors and retirement, with twenty-four-hour security in Prescott Valley, Yavapai County, Arizona.

In 1970, I had written my first original screenplay set in a fictional (based on Sedona) Red Rock, Arizona, and optioned it to James Coburn. I had written an original storyline, now called *Junior Bonner* set at the World's Oldest Rodeo in Prescott.

My Studio City office was again functional. Legitimate. Earl Hamner upstairs. His *The Homecoming: A Novel About Spencer's Mountain* now was optioned to Lorimar in the hopes of a television series to be born from the Christmas special.

While downstairs, in suite 105, paper and carbon into my dad's Royal portable. And the discipline of five and a half days a week of writing became what I had trained myself for since January 1, 1968.

FADE IN. *Junior Bonner* began.

As Joe had ordained, I was immediately thrown into the world that can create success or eventual failure with an original screenplay: collaboration. With Joe, our relationship became positive. I never worried this would be a repeat of *Keeper* and Mark Rydell. From the beginning, Joe and I clicked professionally and personally. Where there were several "based-on" story credits for what became *Jeremiah Johnson* with Milius having to share a rewrite screenplay credit with Edward Anhalt (winner of two Academy Awards: *Panic in the Streets* [1951] won Best Story, Motion Picture, written with Edna Anhalt, one of his five wives, and *Becket* [1964] earned Best

Writing, Screenplay Based on Material from Another Medium), I was thus far flying solo with Joe Wizan.

There are often times in our professional lives when the subtext of a long ago moment kicks in. In my high school days at The Orme School, movies were shown every Friday night. I do not know who chose them, but the 16mm film usually brought us classics. When, within the first ten pages of my screenplay, a bulldozer is shown tearing down Ace Bonner's now-deserted rangeland home to make way for his son Curly's housing development, I realized it came from a Friday night showing of *The Grapes of Wrath* (1940), and a scene where bulldozers arrive upon Oklahoma farmland to assure the displacement of those who had once lived there.

While the bulldozing scene was happening, Junior was on his way back to his hometown of Prescott, setting the stage for the realization of what Curly was doing to the rangeland he had always known.

As a writer of original material, I always experience the really honest anticipation of meeting my characters and immersing them in the drama I am creating. So it was with the eternal dreamer, Ace, whose dreams of wealth following a champion's life in rodeo, seemed to always fail. So it was with his wife, Elvira, who chose to separate from the dream, in lieu of seemingly eternally putting up with his dreams and schemes.

Yes, marriages do fail when dreams are dreamed and then fail.

Now in middle age, Elvira was captured in security by turning the home she once shared with Ace, into an antique shop. The promise was she would run the shop at Curly's retirement community, Sunrise Estates, once it was on its way to becoming a millionaire's reality. Curly had a wife, Ruth, and children—two pre-teen boys and their still-in-her-high-chair sister.

As arranged, when I finished so many pages, usually between ten and fifteen, they were mailed to Joe on location in Utah. I would proceed on. Within a week, Joe would call with his suggestions. If I seemed to be going off course, which did occur early on, he suggested a creative correction. My experience with Mark Rydell proved I was capable of creating strong characters, while being weak on story. Joe Wizan had a strong story sense. Now we both knew my family of characters and a sense of where to take them on our screenplay journey.

The story, which takes place over three days, began to take shape. We already foresaw the ending. Junior had to ride the unrideable bull, Sunshine. That was the third act. Coming home was the first act. On the same wavelength, Joe and I prepared ourselves for a second act.

Writing pages with invented characters is a routine, but what about the reality in Dorothy's eyes, mixed with hope and disappointment? Where was the money to replace worn carpets and other basic needs in our 1,200-square-foot North Hollywood home? As Stuart and Katherine, going on eight and five, grew older, would they live in a house with only one bathroom, one hallway floor heater turned on with a turn-key?

The money to survive was still in our bank account. Solace was my office, working with Joe Wizan with a goal of nabbing Steve McQueen, all the while knowing each day I had left Dorothy behind in a working-class neighborhood where she, college educated, had little in common with the neighbors. She did not want to doubt my opportunity or Joe, yet I had failed before. Disappointment could arrive again.

Maybe I was Junior, who, to find success again within himself, restore self-esteem, had to ride the unrideable Sunshine. Or maybe I was Ace, dreamer of dreams. Dorothy could have been Elvira, once a wife to success, now facing doubts of her husband's dream becoming a failure.

Chasing dreams.

Upon completion of my 1956 paid writing summertime with NBC, I am called into the office of NBC television president Pat Weaver. I am awed, a twenty-one-year-old college senior-to-be, in the presence of a man who created Today *(NBC, 1952-) and* Tonight! *(NBC, 1954-). I am being groomed for* Matinee Theater *(NBC, 1955–1958), a daily live play produced by the network in Los Angeles.*

Chasing dreams.

Dreams implode. "This a very dangerous time," my NBC mentor Nat Wolfe told me two weeks prior to my graduation from Washington and Lee. Code words for he was fired. As was everyone from Pat Weaver on

down in the Sarnoff takeover. At the lowest rung of the corporate debris,
Jeb Rosebrook.

1971

As January became March, quite suddenly Jim Coburn returned
to my life. Director Paul Mielche called to say he and Jim were
traveling to Arizona to look at locations and would I join them?
In spite of all our frustrations with CMA and *Ward Craft* finding
a production date, Paul and I became (and still are) close friends.
Danish-born, raised as an immigrant from World War II in a tough
neighborhood in Oakland, California, an ex-Marine, with college
and short-subject credits behind him, Paul had a firm creative grasp
on *Ward Craft*.

I flew to Phoenix and met them at my mother-in-law's home
in central Phoenix. Let me say this about Jim Coburn, the actor
known as James Coburn. This tall, lean man with a smile that
became the *In Like Flint* (1967) film character, was gracious, modest, and without ego. Our time together, traveling to Prescott, the
Orme Ranch and School, the Upper Bar in Mayer, the landscape of
rangeland in Yavapai County, and even the first Ali-Joe Frazier big
screen fight we attended in Phoenix, was a great and positive time
in my writing life. My rodeo companion, R. Kirk (Sandy) Dunbar
of the previous July, also joined us.

There was hope for *Ward Craft*! Paul Mielche was at work adapt-
ing my screenplay to a workable film. I wondered if the agents at
CMA could sell Jim and the script to a studio and find time for Jim
to make the film. *Or the agency could continue to stall us, and continue*
booking Jim into big-budget action films. I wondered if manager Jim
Logan had the clout to make certain CMA made time for Ward Craft. *I*
prayed James Coburn would be willing to divert his career into a small,
serious, dramatic film and insist to his agents the film be made.

Back to *Junior*.

I had in mind a young woman. She will attend the rodeo and
meet him and dance with him. It will be time out of time for
both of them. Her name came to me, Charmagne. She will work
in a bank in Phoenix. She will be looking for the excitement of

party time, rodeo time, and she will drive up to Prescott in her Volkswagen bug.

Charmagne began to enter the script. She will meet Junior at the Palace Bar and there will be, for them, only for that day and night, their emotional connection, each knowing it was just for the day and the night, and then he will be on his way to the next rodeo and she back to the bank in Phoenix. Every stop of the way had a young woman like Charmagne for Junior. But for Charmagne, it was the excitement of the real deal of a rodeo cowboy—even for a moment, one night, a lasting moment.

But as I wrote them, their connection becomes more than a dance and a one-night stand.

And well into the second act, the important next level characters come alive on the page. The rodeo events brought Junior into competition with his main, and more successful rival, Red Terwiliger. There is Buck Roan, the rodeo stock contractor who owns the never-been-ridden bull, Sunshine. There is Del, the bartender at the Palace. There is Ace's current love interest, Nurse Arlis. Finally, there's an old-timer in the rodeo world, Homer Rutledge.

Add to this, the rodeo circuit barrel-racing twins.

But before the third act, there must be the emotional progression between son and father, Junior and Ace. (Many years later, Joe will reinforce to me that no matter how many wonderful, emotional scenes you write, they must connect emotionally, from beginning to end.)

Ace has his new dream: Australia. He has been looking for silver in Nevada. That dream of riches was only a dream. Returning home to Prescott, he takes to drinking and crashes his pickup truck on the nearby Cherry Creek Road. Hospitalized and in the care of Nurse Arlis, with whom there is a strong attraction, he is told by Curly that there will be no more dreams and schemes. Curly will put him on an allowance. Curly believes he is the dutiful son while, at the same time, planning to have his mother run the forthcoming gift shop at his planned retirement development for senior citizens.

But Ace, to his way of thinking, has another option: Junior. Somehow that scene arrived in my mind: the Prescott train depot. I knew Prescott's Santa Fe, Prescott & Phoenix Railway depot from my many years attending Orme School in the late 1940s. I would be driven to Prescott to board the Santa Fe Railway's "Peavine" passenger train service that operated from Phoenix's Union Station to Ash Fork, where I would connect with the cross-country Santa Fe passenger train back home to New York or Virginia, depending on whether it was winter or summer.

The depot scene will take place after the annual rodeo parade in which Junior and Ace have ridden and participated. Being turned down by Curly, Ace, thinking that Junior is far more successful in rodeo these days than he is, seeks him out to partner with him and bankroll his dream of Australia. The result: Ace learns that Junior is broke. No way can Junior pay his dad's way to the Down Under country. Not even a down payment: "Broke, flatter than a tire," Junior says.

Dramatically and emotionally, Junior and Ace prepare for the third act.

Joe is pleased. I am heading into the third act with numerous plot points to be resolved. The brothers: Junior and Curly—now I am writing that the younger brother wants Junior to give up his rodeo ways, where he is just treading water in a once-promising career, and go to work as a salesman for his Sunrise Estates.

Then there's Ace and his separated wife, Elvira. Will these two always remain apart? Will Arlis steal Ace away?

There is Buck Roan: Junior is honest; he wants to ride that bull. Buck is honest, too. He cannot and won't fix the draw for Junior to ride Sunshine.

And, finally, there will be Charmagne.

Now, for Joe and me, resolving a third act is becoming the magic of knowing your people.

Time is pressing. Joe has been in Utah since January; filming should finish in March.

The Third Act. I do not need to be told there will need to be an emotional connection with, if it is to be, Steve McQueen, the actor, and my family of characters, leading into the third act resolution. Junior and Ace and Australia. Arlis, Elvira, and Ace. Junior and Curly, Junior and Charmagne. Junior and Sunshine.

In the back of my mind, I wonder if all this is very real, about Steve McQueen. There is no action like Steve's car chase in *Bullitt* or on the motorcycle in *The Great Escape* or the race in *Le Mans*.

In the end, against the backdrop of the Palace Bar, Ace must choose between Arlis and Elvira. Junior, in a dance with Charmagne, finds a strong mutual attraction, the romance of the night ahead. In a moment where their lives will meet again, Ace will ask Elvira to share his dream, join him in making a new life in Australia.

Emotion took over. Ace and the triangle, choosing Elvira. Outside, behind the Palace, up the stairs, perhaps the finest and most emotional scene I had ever written. Because there had been love between them, and now only dreams and Australia remained. If their paths are to forever part, there will only be that night.

Dialogue here.

And perhaps in my mind, all those dances in my life, the young women, bodies and cheeks close together, all the music from Country roots, from Hank Williams to Ray Price, and two strangers coming together, Junior and Charmagne, close to the music and the night will be their own. From the music of the late 1960s, the script and I called for the Ian Tyson song, recorded by Judy Collins, "Someday Soon," (w. Ian Tyson) and Merle Haggard's "Today I Started Loving You Again" (w. Merle Haggard and Bonnie Owens).

There still will be the bull, Sunshine.

Ride your bull, Junior.

Spend your night with Charmagne. Good-bye. In a Volkswagen, she drives back to a far less exciting life in Phoenix and the reality of a job in a bank.

Win the money, Junior, send your dad to Australia.

Bid an emotional farewell to your mother.

Say good-bye to your hometown. Shane rides away.

Go down the road. To the next rodeo.

FADE OUT

THE END

I never gave a thought to not having everything wrapped up in the plot, leaving it an open ending. Actually, this was my ending to my story. Everyone will move on to the next phase of their lives. Will Junior come back to Prescott and work for his brother? Will

Director Sam Peckinpah loved making his movies on location with his crew members, and the production of Junior Bonner *in Prescott, Arizona, in the summer of 1971 gave him the opportunity to create one of his best films with select members of the "Peckinpah Company."* Mike Siegel Collection.

ABC Pictures Executive Martin Baum and Joe Wizan's gamble to pair Sam Peckinpah and Steve McQueen in Prescott for the first time since their falling out on The Cincinnati Kid *(1965), allowed the two cinema rebels to rediscover a creative chemistry that led to the creation and release of two of their best films in 1972,* Junior Bonner *and* The Getaway. Mike Siegel Collection.

From the first page to the last of Jeb Rosebrook's original screenplay, Junior Bonner, *Steve McQueen's lead character was center stage, but Wizan and Peckinpah surrounded their star with top professionals, including Academy Award-winner Ben Johnson.* Rosebrook Family Collection.

Leading man Steve McQueen worked with Rodeo Coordinator Casey Tibbs as the star prepped for his part as the aging rodeo star, a role both men, superstars in their own professions respectively—and just a year apart in age—could mutually understand. Rosebrook Family Collection.

Casting Director Lynn Stalmaster must receive a lot of credit for the award-winning cast of co-stars in Junior Bonner, *including Broadway star and Tony Award-winner Robert Preston as Ace Bonner, his first feature-film role since* All the Way Home *(1963).* Rosebrook Family Collection.

While Ida Lupino was not the first actress that Casting Director Lynn Stalmaster invited to test for the role of Elvira Bonner, the veteran actress-director proved a perfect match for the charismatic Preston, and superstar leading man McQueen. Rosebrook Family Collection.

Sam Peckinpah, like John Ford before him, enjoyed working with the Oklahoma cowboy-turned-actor Ben Johnson, and Sam and Ben were reunited in Prescott in 1971 on the set of Junior Bonner, *the first film they had made together since* The Wild Bunch *in 1968.*
Rosebrook Family Collection.

While Joe Don Baker had not appeared on screen with Steve McQueen before the production of Junior Bonner, *McQueen was confident in Baker's casting as his brother, Curly Bonner, from his prior work in McQueen's Solar Production Company film,* Adam at 6 A.M. *(1970).*
Rosebrook Family Collection.

Joe Wizan and Sam Peckinpah originally cast actress Tiffany Boling as Steve McQueen's love interest Charmagne in Junior Bonner, *but on a twist of fate and Hollywood luck, Boling was replaced with the leading man's then-girlfriend Barbara Leigh after production had started in Prescott.*
Rosebrook Family Collection.

On and off the set, rodeo champion Casey Tibbs, the rodeo stunt coordinator and coach to Steve McQueen on Junior Bonner, *brought his sense of levity and humor to the daily production of the film. Casey became a close friend of the Rosebrook family after that summer.* Rosebrook Family Collection.

Bill Pierce
Rodeo Chairman

*Without Arizona Film Commission agent and Prescott Jaycee Rodeo Chairman Bill Pierce's knowledge of the Prescott and Yavapai County business community—and his ability to work with Sam Peckinpah's prickly personality—*Junior Bonner *may not have ever been made, at least not in Prescott, Arizona.* Rosebrook Family Collection.

Steve McQueen, who personally helped age Junior's Cadillac convertible, was an actor who took pride in the sparcity of his on-camera dialogue. The quarry scenes in which he witnesses the destruction of the family homestead and his showdown with the construction worker and his front-loader, includes fewer than a half-dozen lines of dialogue and are one of the most effective sequences in the picture. Rosebrook Family Collection.

Curly Bonner's under-value purchase of the Bonner Family homestead, and its subsequent destruction to make way for retirement homes, is one of the most symbolically laden scenes in Junior Bonner. *Ironically, the production company was able to acquire an old ranch house scheduled for demolition to make way for actual development near the new town of Prescott Valley, Arizona.* Mike Siegel Collection.

Producer Joe Wizan (right) worked closely with Peckinpah and McQueen during pre-production in Prescott, and was a regular on the set during the first half of location production, including the scenes at the quarry, before he left to begin pre-production on his next film, Prime Cut.
Mike Siegel Collection.

Like a captain of a ship, director Sam Peckinpah was the ultimate choreographer on his set, one reason he mostly chose to direct scripts that demanded they be made on location to be true to their screenplays.
Mike Siegel Collection.

The fact that McQueen's Solar Production Company was invested in the film—and that the leading man was also the highest-paid movie star in the world in 1971—gave McQueen the authority to share his opinions about his role and the production of Junior Bonner *with Sam on the set, a privilege not every star was afforded on a Peckinpah film.* Mike Siegel Collection.

Location Manager Bill Pierce acquired the use of a Prescott Valley gravel pit, which gave Sam the realism he demanded for his productions, and one of the most challenging locations of the summer for the crew and cast.
Mike Siegel Collection.

*Peckinpah directs his camera crew as McQueen shouts to the driver of the
front-loader during the challenging sequences at the gravel pit.*
Mike Siegel Collection.

*Peckinpah used Junior Bonner's Cadillac convertible with horse-trailer in tow
as a symbol of the aging rodeo champion cowboy's vagabond life was nearing
an end—a future visualized with the destruction of the family ranch.*
Mike Siegel Collection.

When the summer monsoon rains turned the natural dust of the quarry into mud and threatened the production schedule of the film, Peckinpah turned to his location manager Bill Pierce for a solution. Pierce saved the day when he had his friend who owned the quarry deliver three truckloads of gravel dust. Mike Siegel Collection.

A signature of Sam Peckinpah films is recruiting local residents featured in key supporting roles and as extras. One memorable local cast member in Junior Bonner *was the front-end loader driver, who Sam is coaching before they film his showdown with McQueen and his Cadillac.* Mike Siegel Collection.

McQueen, like Sam, had a great respect for working men and women, and
Junior Bonner*'s leading man spent quality time with the local heavy-*
equipment operator cast as his nemesis in the famous quarry showdown.
Mike Siegel Collection.

Sam Peckinpah was a master of choreography on his location sets, directing his
crew to film the coverage he needed to edit the film into its final sequence in
the editing room. The duel between the modern "construction cowboy" and his
front-end loader and the aging "rodeo cowboy" and his Cadillac convertible is
Sam Peckinpah movie magic at its best. Mike Siegel Collection.

At the heart of the Junior Bonner *screenplay is a story of a dysfunctional family, a major reason why both Sam Peckinpah and Steve McQueen immediately connected with the script and agreed to direct and star in the project.* Mike Siegel Collection.

Sam's direction of the pre-rodeo family dinner scene at Ida Lupino/Elvira Bonner's home, with McQueen, and Mary Murphy as Ruth Bonner, Junior's sister-in-law, is one of his finest choreographies of multiple stars in one scene in the movie. Most critics would also agree that the two leading ladies, Murphy and Lupino, steal the dinner table scene from their higher-paid male co-stars, McQueen and Baker. Mike Siegel Collection.

McQueen and Baker carefully rehearsed and choreographed their fraternal fight on the family porch, which results in one of the most memorable lines delivered by Baker's Curly Bonner character: "What a salesman you'd make for the Rancheros! Big Cowboy like you. Sincere. Genuine as a sunshine."
Rosebrook Family Collection.

Junior want to make his relationship with Charmagne more than a brief affair? Will Elvira decide to be with Ace on his new journey to live Down Under?

Former Paramount executive Dan Bowman points to open endings of that period, from Altman's "It don't worry me" ending of *Nashville* (1975) to Ben and Elaine sitting silently on a bus together in *The Graduate* (1967) to Robert Towne's encapsulating final words in *Chinatown* (1974)—"Forget it, Jake, it's Chinatown." *The Italian Job* (1969) starring Michael Caine was another brilliant example of a film with an open ending from that era. It's mostly dead from cinema today because everybody wants a happy ending. I was glad to see it was briefly revived with Woody Allen's *Blue Jasmine* (2013), leaving Cate Blanchett on a bus-stop bench in San Francisco.

It is March and there are no more suggestions. Joe is satisfied. He is still in Utah, but he will now go about planning the business approach to the screenplay.

There is silence on *Ward Craft* and Jim Coburn.

Wait, there is one more rewrite. Joe has returned from Utah; he has met with his former CMA mentor, Martin (Marty) Baum, now heading up ABC Pictures.

Joe could not have a stronger mentor than Marty. As an agent with CMA, Baum represented a litany of major actors, directors, and writers. Now forty-seven years old and steering ABC Pictures, with *Cabaret* (1972) and *Straw Dogs* (1971) in production overseas, and the Academy Award-winning film *They Shoot Horses, Don't They?* (1969) to his credit, Martin Baum is at the prime of his game as a studio head.

Baum suggests small dramatic changes in the final scene's dialogue between Ace and Elvira. If this is to be their final moment, it must be powerful and memorable, to heighten the drama to raw emotions between the two of them and Ace's exit to Australia.

In the midst of hope or failure, with money and Stuart and Katherine and our future always in mind, Dorothy had broken down, asking how much more of this we could both take. We were at home having lunch. In frustration I picked up my plate and hurled it into the wall, shattering it into pieces. And then I stood before my wife, ashamed, and she in silence.

A writer's high of completing his or her screenplay can very soon turn to the increasing anxiety of waiting. I was fortunate that Joe had already given me his notes as we'd built the screenplay, plot point by plot point, and scene by scene, from beginning to end. I did not suffer the writer paranoia of waiting for notes, that my script might get rewritten, or that I'd have to share, or even worse, lose my hard-earned credit, as many screenwriters did in the Hollywood writing game.

March became April.

There was still Wizan money in the bank. The option period was but five months old. Paul Mielche was near completing his shooting script for *Ward Craft*. Stuart would soon turn eight, Katherine was four going toward five. Each day they walked to nearby Burbank Elementary School. Their teachers were wonderful. Dorothy, whose teaching career expired at Encino Elementary due to pregnancy, was volunteering with the PTA. She had been active at our Saint David's Episcopal Church until a schism with a rumored talking-in-tongues vestry accused Dorothy of not bringing enough Jesus to the Sunday School she headed up.

A positive change was definitely in order for the Rosebrook family living at 12301 Collins Street, North Hollywood, California, 91607.

How often do important things in your life happen out of the blue? What no one expected, taking you off guard?

"Joe called," Dorothy told me, as I returned from the office for lunch. "You're to pick him up. You're going to Steve McQueen's house tonight."

And so it was. To the McQueen home in Brentwood. Ring the buzzer. The gate opens.

Neile McQueen, in her late thirties, married to the highest-paid movie star in the world, is preparing dinner for the couple's two children, Chad, eleven, and Terry, twelve.

Life goes on in the kitchen. Joe and I take a seat in an adjacent den. (But how does life go on, when only months before, during the making of *Le Mans* [1971], Neile, taking cocaine at her husband's insistence, has his gun to her head when she admits to an entwining moment with actor Maximilian Schell?)

Steve enters. Like Coburn, Steve is a client of CMA. He is now forty years old. While not tall, his build is lean. His eyes riveting. I am introduced. I sit beside Joe but the attention of the highest-paid movie star in the world is on Joe.

Steve gets right down to the business of the script. Years later I remember little of what his points were, other than he really liked the script! In the midst of this, he turns his eyes on me, then turning to Joe.

"Doesn't he take notes?" McQueen asked.

Oh, shit! But Joe quickly exudes his usual manner of Wizan confidence. "Jeb always remembers."

Apparently satisfied for the moment, Steve returns to his positive thoughts on my screenplay. (Years later I will realize that Jeb Rosebrook might well be only a starting point as a writer, given the number of writers McQueen caused to be brought in on his other films, including *Bullitt*.)

Steve is satisfied. He has confidence in the man I will come to call "The Wizard of Wizan." After a half-hour, the meeting concludes. Steve is relaxed.

Joe and I stop at Ship's coffee shop in Westwood. Joe is cautious but feeling strong.

I drop Joe off at an apartment in Los Angeles—temporary quarters upon his return from Utah and, I soon learn, an impending split with his first wife, Barbara.

Joe had placed his faith, and his investment partners' money, in me. Our partnership had also become a bond of friendship.

I came home with the good news.

"Steve likes the script, Dorothy. Enough to make the movie." But fifty thousand dollars, only if it becomes a movie.

What I did not know that night as Joe and I sat at Ship's was that Joe knew he had found Steve McQueen at his most vulnerable. *Le Mans* was a financial disaster, with Steve as the producer and star. His marriage to Neile was crumbling. (Oh, how many years had she looked the other way with all his affairs, dalliances and one-night stands?)

Le Mans, this disaster, his last picture, the ashes still smoldering.

I remember Mike Wise's call: "Robert Redford is looking for a rodeo script."

"The World's Oldest Rodeo" is ten weeks away. I had written the script for Prescott. The average pre-production time in preparing a film is eight to twelve weeks. We are ten weeks away. Steve will soon sign. (I believe!) But there is no location scouting. Beyond Steve, there is no cast and, importantly, there is no director. What we have are Steve, Joe, me, and—I now learn—what I had suspected: Marty Baum and ABC Pictures.

The saying in Hollywood is that producers and directors are egomaniacs; actors are children; and writers are paranoid. What if Joe and Marty want to wait beyond Prescott's rodeo? New Mexico had recently been the location for another CMA/Mike Wise client, director/writer Steve Innes, and a rodeo film, *The Honkers* (1972)— ironically, with Jim Coburn. For the Rosebrook family on Collins Street in North Hollywood, fifty thousand dollars will not contractually come our way until production begins.

Within ten days, Joe calls.

"We have a director."

"Who?"

"Sam Peckinpah."

Sam Peckinpah!

Joe tells me Sam had completed filming *Straw Dogs* in England. My mind went back a few years earlier. Earl Hamner and I had taken an evening to go see *The Wild Bunch* (1969). When we emerged from the theater we both agreed, no one will be making a Western for long time. Sam Peckinpah and his cinematographer, Lucien Ballard, had taken the essence of John Ford's skies and land, the legend of what was the West, and turned it on its ugly head— men who are out of step with time in the early twentieth century. A more violent film had never been made: slow-motion violence, an opening with children torturing a scorpion in an ant hill and then setting the death-match ablaze; a young Mexican's throat cut right before our eyes, and dialogue, as a young Bo Hopkins, one of the outlaws in William Holden's gang, shouts defiantly at his executioners, "You can kiss my mother's black cat's ass!"

Soon Sam Peckinpah, forty-five, and I were sitting side-by-side before Marty Baum. One of us borrowed a Marlboro from the other. I cannot remember which of us it was. We smoked. His hazel eyes alternately eyed Marty and me. I was well aware of his reputation, going back to his rewrite of *Ride the High Country* (1962) and genius casting of old-timers Randolph Scott and Joel McCrea, the award-winning adaptation of Katherine Anne Porter's *Noon Wine* (ABC, 1967) for *ABC Stage 67* (ABC, 1966-1967), and his industry black-balling resulting from the production-plagued *Major Dundee* (1965). In order to see Peckinpah's latest, Dorothy and I had gone to see Robert Altman's *McCabe and Mrs. Miller* (1971). Warner Brothers had dumped *The Ballad of Cable Hogue* (1970) to be second-billing of a double feature. We were so happily pleased with Jason Robards as Cable and his screen story, we left without seeing *McCabe and Mrs. Miller*.

What I also knew was that Sam Peckinpah was, unlike Mark Rydell, a writer, who learned from his earlier years on television Westerns, including *Gunsmoke* (CBS, 1955-1975), *The Rifleman* (ABC, 1958–1963), and his own short-lived series, *The Westerner* (NBC, 1960).

Sam was a slightly built, mustached man who was ten years older than me. Although he appeared relaxed, he seemed coiled. This was underscored by his soft-spoken tone and the appraising eyes—as if a gambler, waiting for me to show my cards first.

Marty Baum was dividing his time now to prepare *Junior Bonner* and the European completion of *Cabaret*. He and Sam had worked together on *Straw Dogs*, and there appeared to me to be a creative trust between them.

Two years later during the Writers Guild strike of 1973, I would walk the picketing line beside James Poe, who had won an Academy Award for *Lilies of the Field* (1963) a decade earlier. He carried his own hand-painted sign, which proclaimed "Without the Word There is Nothing!" Here I was, with the words, which in the collaborative world of filmmaking, had given birth, but only birth. And only incidentally, Marty was the agent behind Sidney Poitier and *Lilies of the Field* as he was behind *They Shoot Horses, Don't They?* (1969) on which Poe was also the writer.

There was now the immediate task of casting with the urgency of but five weeks if we were to film in Prescott at the Frontier Days Rodeo.

Sam then invited me to join him and Marty to look at the editing progress on *Straw Dogs*.

It was my first Peckinpah test, said the spider to the fly! While Marty and ABC executive Lew Rachmil sat in the back, I sat beside Sam to view the most violent anal rape scene (by two men) against actress Susan George. When the lights came up, Sam was clearly delighted. Marty and Lou were confident that Sam would use the scene as the basis of editing by Roger Spottiswoode. Sam smiled.

What did I think? I had to filter my words carefully.

I said it was a very powerful scene. I mean two English rednecks taking turns! (What I did not know until years later, from David Weddle's exceptional biography of Sam, "*If They Move... Kill 'Em!*", was that the strong physical and emotional entwinement had poured out and into Sam's sexually charged, anguished, angry rewrite of *Straw Dogs*.) The rape scene in *Straw Dogs* leaves little to the imagination in its graphic detail of actress Susan George.

I drove home.

"How was he?" Dorothy asked that evening. I told her he had filmed the most violent rape scene ever in the history of movies.

"And?"

"We got along."

"And?"

"We have a star and a director. Now we need a cast."

Five weeks. If we make the picture in Prescott.

Marty, Joe, Steve, and Sam wasted little time. Joe, Steve, and Sam spent a weekend at Steve's Palm Springs home going over the script. The notes from that meeting were transcribed, typed, and waiting for me at the Century City office of ABC Pictures. The date was May 31. One month to filming.

Generally, the notes followed the story within the script but went deeper into Junior's motivations, infusing a richer tone to the screenplay. The notes included mentions of Gene Hackman as Curly and Robert Preston to play Ace.

The trio of Marty, Joe, and Sam, including me and excluding Steve, moved quickly on the casting. As the virgin within our group, I listened to what I found to be the casting genius of Marty Baum. Marty believed the father and mother roles, Ace and Elvira, must be cast with strong talent to push Steve beyond his usual starring roles in which he always rose above the cast members around him, making him the total dramatic center of attention. Marty used the example of Paul Newman in *Hud* (1963) for which Patricia Neal and Melvyn Douglas each won Academy Awards for Supporting Actors.

There was a rhythm to Ace Bonner's dialogue and charm to his dreamer ways that led Marty to an easy choice, Robert Preston. Bob, as I would later know him, at fifty-three, was a household name to both film and Broadway audiences for his role as Professor Harold Hill in Meredith Wilson's *The Music Man* (1962). With the exception of service as an intelligence officer in the Army Air Corps during World War II, Preston had never been out of work as an actor since his film debut with Paramount in 1938. His Broadway career had earned him two Tony Awards for *The Music Man* (Broadway, 1957–1961) and *I Do, I Do* (Broadway, 1966–1968).

Not only was Bob Preston available for the role of Ace, but he eagerly accepted.

Steve's reaction: "I'm going to be working with Preston Foster?" referring to an actor well-known for mostly B-starring roles.

The casting of Ace's separated wife, Elvira, turned out far differently.

Marty flew Susan Hayward out from her home in Florida. At fifty-four, the Brooklyn-born Hayward had been acting in films since the late 1930s, rising to stardom to win an Academy Award in 1959 for *I Want to Live!* (1958). She hadn't done a film in nearly five years, and this role could be a great comeback vehicle.

Preston and Hayward. Marty Baum's vision.

Marty arranged a meet-and-greet luncheon with the actress at the Beverly Wilshire Hotel. Joe still did not have a car. Sam would meet us there. Our Plymouth station wagon (on which I was making lease payments on a loan from Dorothy's mother) was pressed into service, complete with Kleenexes strewn about the floor of the backseat, used by our allergy-plagued daughter, Katherine.

Our luncheon with the vivacious Susan Hayward was a total thrill for me. Sam and Joe led the conversation, which largely, almost entirely, revolved around her long and honored career. Sam's only experience with an actress of Susan's stature had been Maureen

O'Hara in his first feature, *The Deadly Companions* (1961). That relationship, I would learn, did not end well for Sam. Was Susan Hayward aware of this? Meanwhile, Joe spoke glowingly of her past accomplishments. As for me, I finally asked, "May I call you Susan?" She replied as one who was Brooklyn-born, "That's my name." We assumed Marty had made the proper arrangements to sign her, if he had not already.

Our luncheon concluded with warm good-byes, certain we would soon be seeing Susan Hayward as Elvira Bonner.

But what we did not know was that Susan Hayward felt less than appreciated.

"She's on a plane back to Florida!" reacted an angry, perplexed Marty Baum when we reported in to his office after lunch. "You never once brought up the goddamn script!"

The best reply we could summon: "She never brought the script and her part up to us. We assumed..."

What next?

Marty thought quickly.

Ida Lupino.

Well-known for her long and distinguished acting career, Ida Lupino was also known as a pioneering woman director. English-born, her American acting career began at Paramount in 1933. While she was never a headline star, she had worked with top film directors and actors through the forties and into the fifties. She showed a real spirit and virtuosity by directing a succession of indie-produced films and found herself in television, as actress, director, and producer of *Mr. Adams and Eve* (CBS, 1957–1958) with her husband, Howard Duff.

Let me say that Ida Lupino had a *presence*. Whereas Susan Hayward was clearly a movie star, beautiful and sexy at fifty-four, Ida, also fifty-four, carried a sense of her own beauty and the presence of one who had accomplished it all in film and television. There was not one ounce of insecurity about her.

Except, being called into a reading at very short notice, she slurred her lines in the reading. Is she drunk? No, she apologized, the Novocain was wearing off from a dentist's appointment before joining us at Marty's Century City office.

She wanted the part, and she got it. And she was exceptional, too.

But there was also the script and the urgency of time if the script was to be filmed in Prescott, for where it was written. We were entering May. The World's Oldest Rodeo kicked off with an annual parade on June 30.

Steve, Joe, and Sam spent another weekend at Steve's place in Palm Springs. They discussed the script in detail, scene by scene.

Their two days together were set down on a tape recorder and then transcribed: "JUNIOR BONNER. Conversations between Steve McQueen, Sam Peckinpah, and Joe Wizan."

It began with Steve leading the charge: "Well, the only thing Curly brings to mind to me is that I had a scene in mind of when I go to Mom's house and I have that scene with her, which could be outside carrying the tomatoes into the kitchen and she'd be kinda marvelous, which I'd like to get into, but at any rate, it's kinda drop it on her, 'Where's Curly at?' 'cause I think, at that point, Junior is starting to build up what the fuck happened."

And so it went for fifty-five nonstop pages. The tape-recorded reels went to ABC Pictures in Century City, where they were quickly and urgently typed up.

The pages came to me shortly, on May 31. I had digested those fifty-five pages into just over five pages of single-spaced typewritten notes and additional notes from Joe: *JUNIOR BONNER OUTLINE FOR SCRIPT REVISIONS: As per Joe Wizan to Jeb Rosebrook based upon notes and tapes, meeting with McQueen, Sam Peckinpah, Joe Wizan.*

We were now officially Junior Bonner Productions. Joe moved our pre-production office to the CBS lot (once Republic Studios) in Studio City. This was less than ten minutes from our North Hollywood home. With Joe, came Betty Gumm, his secretary and assistant. As I came to know her, Betty was not just essential to Joe's life, but an absolutely wonderful person. Sam added his assistant, a beautiful young English woman, Katy Haber, who had not only been Sam's assistant on *Straw Dogs*, but had become his lover.

I walked with Sam to a nearby Studio City Mexican restaurant adjacent to the studio. Up until now, our relationship had been growing closer, but only on creative terms with the script. Sam casually mentioned, "I hit Joie last night." I had never met Joie Gould, but learned she was zeroing in on becoming Sam's third wife. They had been together in England. But then came Katy.

He waited for my reaction. Was this a confession to let me know what kind of a man he was? We hardly knew one another.

"I hit Joie last night."

I recall saying nothing but perhaps, "Jesus, Sam." I had never met a man who hit a woman, much less confessed it openly. The subject changed. We had lunch. With a scheduled trip to look at a location, we were going to Prescott, Sam was bringing me in, after I'd learned up front more than I needed to know.

A confession or a warning? Certainly another one of his tests.

It all happened so fast. Dorothy was taking Katherine and Stuart to Texas to her younger brother Bill's wedding. I could not attend, as I was bound for Prescott. Stuart suddenly came down with a twisted testicle, which needed an operation. Surgery was postponed until after the wedding. Medicated for pain and wearing a new blue blazer, Jeb Stuart Rosebrook was on his way to Texas together with his mom and sister.

Dad was on Western Airlines, LAX to Phoenix, a late afternoon flight. Joe Wizan, his best friend and associate producer Mickey Barofsky, cinematographer Lucien Ballard, wrangler Kenny Lee, Katy Haber, Sam, and me. Sam had been working all day with editor Roger Spotiswoode and arrived clearly exhausted. He learned that, in violation of Directors Guild contractual rules requiring only first-class travel (as well as Writers Guild), we were all coach.

Sam was last to board. There was no first class.

He let Joe know in more than anger. If ABC was so cheap to send Sam Peckinpah coach, then they would pay for it.

And pay, they did. Upon arrival in Phoenix, there would be no travel to Prescott. There would be dinner on ABC. And Joe Wizan and Marty Baum will be stuck with the bill.

Somehow a fine, expensive restaurant was found. There were drinks for all (Joe was not a drinker), including champagne. Steaks and lobster were ordered—an exorbitant, expensive meal for all.

What next?

"Let's talk," Sam said to me in the bar of the motel where we all encamped for the night before heading for Prescott the next day.

It had been less than a year since R. Kirk (Sandy) Dunbar and I had attended the Frontier Days Rodeo, and on the return drive to Phoenix, the change in the landscape from rangeland to housing developments on the outskirts of Prescott, the pioneering new Town of Prescott Valley rising across the land, had given me an inspiration for the story that became "Bonner" and now a nearly finished screenplay titled *Junior Bonner*, starring the highest-paid actor in the world, Steve McQueen.

Sam drank brandy straight. He voiced no anger, only a threat. This slender man with the mustache was now not just a comrade in creativity, but a director with but a month and change to begin filming—if he was convinced the movie was to be made in Prescott. And he needed a completed script ready to shoot.

"If you can't do it," he said, "I'll tie a tin can to your ass and mail you home."

I was not fazed by his threat. Hell, it was my story. I had come this far. I was going home to Prescott. I told him I was here to do what was needed and on time.

Sam Peckinpah considered this as he finished the brandy. Then he went out to the motel swimming pool. Fully clothed, he dove in.

I called Dorothy early the next morning. The wedding party was doing fine and Stuart was holding up in spite of the pain. Then I called Joe to tell him I was ready for Prescott. Somehow, the call went not to Joe's room but to Sam. Sam was no doubt performing a sexual exorcism on his hangover with Katy. I could only say I would be ready for travel when he was ready. When we hung up, I thought perhaps there was a tin can waiting to be tied to my ass and mailed home.

"I hit Joie." Okay, but who really was Katy?

Before Sam discovered his WD (wandering dick) and as his fame was jumping from television to feature film, there was his first wife, Marie, the one woman in his life I would never meet. Marie, as introduced in David Weddle's biography, was the Fresno State beauty and stage actress who captured Sam's heart at college, and into a marriage that produced three children, Sharon, Kristen, and

Matthew. They found one another in the love of theater and Sam's achievements in directing John Steinbeck's *Of Mice and Men* and Tennessee Williams's *The Glass Menagerie*.

Weddle also mentions that Marie found it odd (uncomfortable?) how Sam, when visiting his mother, would spend private time only with her.

Marie was over. I had yet to meet Joie Gould.

The nearly two-hour drive north on Interstate 17, and west on State Highway 69 to Prescott was a total adventure in collaborative creativity. Sam and I sat side-by-side in the back with Katy on his other side, taking notes. She never interrupted; she listened and she wrote.

Then, I knew only that Katy had been imported from England and *Straw Dogs* to join Sam on *Junior Bonner*. It was not until reading Weddle's biography that I learned Sam had already hit Katy.

Whatever is said of Sam Peckinpah, when he had the desire to be on his game as director and writer for his vision of a film, he proved himself a generous genius. By the time we reached Prescott, we had been through every scene in the screenplay and we played with dialogue in all of them. In the scene at the Santa Fe Depot, he inserted his whorehouse lines about being snowed in in Nevada, which complemented my line of whatever happened to Bob Cox—stolen with pleasure from my fraternity brother Dan Cox who boasted, "As long as my name lives, sex will never die."

If I looked forward to meeting the mayor and city officials at a dinner that night, I was to be bluntly disappointed. Sam had ordered paper and a typewriter to my motel room.

"You are goddamn well going nowhere except to the rewrite."

When the command was given, Sam waited a moment as if I wished to fight back on the decision. He was coiled but never struck. No tin can tied to my ass tonight. I went to writing. I wrote the next day as Sam, Katy, Joe, Mickey, Lucien, and production manager Jim Pratt went to look for locations with Kenny Lee.

But it was left to William (Bill) Pierce, a Prescott insurance executive, chairman of the Prescott Rodeo Fair Association Committee and Arizona Film Commission representative for the town, to seal the deal to have ABC Pictures commit to making the film in Prescott when he met with Sam, Jim Pratt, and several others (probably Lucien and

Katy) at the Prescottonian Motel. Pierce remembers: "Sam was lying on the bed and a bottle of Martel brandy was on the nightstand with a glass half full beside it." Pierce waited in a long silence. "He [Peckinpah] never acknowledged my presence."

Up to this time, Prescott was an undiscovered gem of a town and countryside for filming, giving way to the red rocks of Sedona, where so many recognizable Westerns had been made. Tom Mix had a ranch in Prescott from 1912 until 1915 and filmed many silent movies here, even competing in what was now known as The World's Oldest Rodeo. Tim McCoy and Buck Jones had come to Prescott to film *Arizona Bound* (1941) when the town had a small Western set for filming ventures.

Pierce broke the silence, telling Sam he had better things to do. Finally, a reaction and a decision from the brandy-drinking man on the bed: "I am going with this guy and the rest of you fuckers can follow."

We left Prescott for Los Angeles. That weekend in the Prescott newspaper, under the headline of "North Vietnam Rockets Strike Da Nang," was a sidebar headline: "McQueen to be in film, rodeo parade here." Joe had Mickey Barofsky make the announcement: "The movie, *Junior Bonner*, will co-feature Robert Preston, famed star of *The Music Man*, who will play McQueen's father."

The announcement continued: "The movie will concern a cowboy from Prescott and it will be about Prescott." Barofsky said, "Prescott's real name will be used in the movie. We won't conjure up an imaginary name for the city."

Back in my Studio City office, determined that no Sam Peckinpah was going to tie a tin can to my ass, I plunged into the script revisions.

By week's end, they were completed and handed in to Sam, Joe, and Marty.

Casting continued. Casting Director Lynn Stallmaster was the single most successful casting director in film and television (*Gunsmoke*) but more importantly, in film. At forty-four, his casting credits were a "Who's Who" of important Hollywood films. Joe had recently used him for *Jeremiah Johnson* and Steve pressed him into service on *The Thomas Crown Affair* a few years prior. Lynn was personable and professional, and my time spent with him was to prove a valuable professional learning experience.

Who will play Junior's brother, Curly? It came down to Texas-born Joe Don Baker, who was thirty-five years old at the time. Joe Don had a recent starring role in a small independent film, *Adam at Six A.M.* (1970), and he had made a name as a formidable television villain in such series as *Mod Squad* (ABC, 1968–1973). A more-than-serious actor with a large physical presence, Joe Don was a graduate of the Actor's Studio in New York. In *Adam at Six A.M.*, a film in which Steve's company, Solar Productions had a stake, Joe Don got a breakthrough as a credited third lead in Michael Doug-las's initial starring role. Joe Don was an actor on the way up. His initial film debut was an uncredited part in *Cool Hand Luke* (1967). Joe Don got the part of Curly.

For the role of Charmagne, I envisioned a young, attractive blonde, up from her day-to-day bank job in Phoenix, looking for fun and action on a Prescott rodeo weekend. What better place to spend a good time than the Fourth of July along Prescott's famed Whiskey Row?

A young actress, twenty-five-year-old Tiffany Bolling, not only read well for the part, but there seemed unanimous consent in the room after she left the reading that we had found our Charmagne. This would be her big break, playing opposite Steve. Tiffany, who grew up in Santa Monica had begun her career with appearances on *Bonanza* (NBC, 1959–1973), *The Mod Squad*, and as cast member of the short-lived television series *The New People* (ABC, 1969–1970) about a group of teenagers stranded on a deserted island.

Coming in to read right after Tiffany was a slender, stylish bru-nette, Georgia-born Barbara Leigh, also twenty-five. Barbara was a high-profile fashion model with very little acting experience. I did not envision her dancing in my arms in the Palace—too unobtain-able. Her reading was just that, an okay reading.

Barbara left. The discussion centered only around Tiffany for the role of Charmagne, yet I do recall catching Steve looking out the window as Barbara made her way toward her car in the studio lot.

Between casting calls, I was getting to know Steve better. He was including me in his conversations with Joe and Sam. Waiting for the elevator on our way to Joe's and the production offices, I remember Steve dissing himself about his part in *The Thomas Crown Affair* three years earlier, admitting to initially not knowing his lines too well until up against Faye Dunaway, who took her role, like her lines, more than seriously.

For me, still the outsider, this reminded me of a story in *Variety* announcing the film and questioning what will happen when Steve is under Sam's direction. The point being raised was what role, if any, he had in in getting Sam fired off *The Cincinnati Kid*, thus providing a pivotal beginning to Canadian Norman Jewison's career

Quickly enough, Lynn brought in Bill McKinney to read for the part of Red Terwiliger, Junior's rodeo rival, in life and in sport. Bill had made a name for himself as the backwoods heavy in *Deliverance* (1972) sodomizing Ned Beatty. Craggy face, muscular and with riveting eyes, McKinney, a Tennessee native was now almost forty years old and an actor who had paid his Hollywood dues: from Korean War Navy veteran to acting classes at the Pasadena Playhouse and, like Joe Don, the Actor's Studio, to being a professional arborist to ten years as a middle school teacher. Just as quickly as he read for the part, Bill McKinney was Red Terwiliger.

Sam knew there was only one choice for Buck Roan, the rodeo stock contractor—Ben Johnson. As if the violent, idyllic beauty of *The Wild Bunch* as filmed by Sam and Lucien Ballard were not so visibly likened to the Western skies and land of John Ford, Ben Johnson, no matter what is said of John Wayne and Ward Bond, was indelibly identified with Ford. Ford loved this Oklahoma cowboy for the way he sat a horse and made certain, within his cavalry trilogy, there were moments when the camera simply captured the grace of Ben Johnson on horseback.

The problem was money. Word was circulating throughout Hollywood about Ben's role in the filmed adaptation of Larry McMurtry's novel, *The Last Picture Show* (1971). This was why his agent felt Ben was worth no less than $5,000 a week. Ben came in to chat with Sam and Joe. We talked about our experiences in the most recent earthquake. Ben lived in Sylmar where the dam broke and he remembered damn near being clobbered by his dresser toppling over. I remembered, too, being so scared that I jumped out of bed and held onto the doorframes in our bedroom while peeing in my pants.

There was no talk of money. A former World Champion team roper, Ben was hardly a stranger to rodeo. It was only a matter of $5,000 a week—and, as it turned out, a small part for his nephew, Ben Miller. Five thousand a week, it was.

As for the part of Curly's wife, Sam also made this call: Mary Murphy. Now forty years old, Mary Murphy was an on-screen love of mine in *The Wild One* (1953), the biker picture I saw five times in which Brando finds his challenge in small-town girl Mary Murphy. (I will later learn Sam had known Mary with intimacy as he rose through the television ranks as writer and director, during her short-lived marriage to actor Dale Robertson.)

Marty made the call on casting Preston's squeeze, Nurse Arlis. (She never had a first name!) Sandra Deel, forty-four, was a singer/actress from New York with Broadway roots. When her part was ready to film, she would be flown out from New York.

Then the remainder of the parts:

Sam made the call for Dub Taylor to play the part of the bartender at the Palace Bar. Dub, too, had worked with Sam as the temperance preacher in the opening sequence of *The Wild Bunch*. Virginia-born and Georgia-raised, Dub had spent popular B-Western movie days known as "Cannonball" and a sidekick to Charles Starrett, Raymond Hatton, Jimmy Wakely, and "Wild Bill" Elliott. On the more serious side, he had been a favorite of Frank Capra's, who cast him in small parts in *You Can't Take It With You* (1938) and *Mister Smith Goes to Washington* (1939). Dub Taylor was now sixty-four years old.

Memories of being a kid who rarely missed a B-Western movie were triggered one lunchtime when I was alone in the production office. There was one man waiting to read for the part of the older, retired rodeo cowboy, Homer Rutledge.

"Hello," I said.

"Hello, I'm Bob Steele." Bob Steele! One of my B-movie cowboy heroes! Bob Steele was now sixty-four years old, a bandy rooster at five-feet-five. Steele was also a serious actor in roles in *Of Mice and Men* (1939), *The Big Sleep* (1946), and other high-profile films.

In my advertising days, copy writer Dave Field and art director Jack Johnson helped put on "The Charles Starrett Film Festival," featuring a cartoon and the Durango Kid himself, ironically with "Cannonball" Dug Taylor as his sidekick. Shown in the back patio of our North Hollywood home, the initial offering was such a success, we followed it with "The Charles Starrett Film Festival Salutes Bob Steele." A keg of beer and a flick. Enough of a crowd attended that some sat on the edge of our roof, including Margaret O'Brien, married to one of the agency's art directors.

Steve would make the decision in favor of an even shorter bandy rooster, Don "Red" Barry. Don "Red" was fifty-nine years old, a one-time Texas college football player who had come to fame (and given his nickname of "Red") in the Republic Pictures serial *The Adventures of Red Ryder* (1940), and subsequent B Westerns throughout the 1940s and, like Bob Steele, found work in television and films in future years in smaller guest roles. But he had a talent for writing and several films were made from his story talent, as well as his talent as director of the cult B Western, *Jesse James' Women* (1954).

Again in the production office: "Hello, I'm Casey Tibbs." Anyone who knew rodeo knew of the great bronc rider, up to that time the greatest of them all, South Dakota's world champion, now forty-three years old, heavier than in his prime and with a mustache, but not without the self-assured swagger that placed him in 1951 as the only professional rodeo cowboy to ever grace the cover of *Life* magazine.

Joe and Sam had hired the one-and-only Casey as our rodeo consultant together with Mickey Gilbert (later of *Fall Guy* [ABC, 1981-1986] fame) as stunt coordinator and well-known rodeo great and now stunt man, Ross Dollarhide. Like Casey, Ross had a youthful, superb, precocious talent for rodeo, enough to leave cowboy ranching for cowboy rodeo. By 1953 he was a world champion steer wrestler. Due to an injury he would leave the rodeo circuit and, like Casey, find plentiful work as a stuntman in film and television, including the outstanding Tom Gries-directed Western, *Will Penny* (1967), occasionally doubling for James Arness in *Gunsmoke*, and just months before with Jim Coburn in the rodeo film, *The Honkers* (1972). Quiet and soft spoken, Ross was the real deal.

We had three 1953 world champions on the film: Ben (team roping), Casey (bronc riding), and Ross (steer wrestling.)

Not long after my thirty-fifth birthday we headed to Prescott for a week of rehearsals prior to filming beginning with the June 30 Frontier Days Rodeo Parade. Our son, Stuart, would be off to the Orme School's Summer Camp near Prescott and once we began filming, Dorothy and Katherine would follow for a visit.

Just before leaving Los Angeles I went to the offices of Creative Management Associates on Beverly Boulevard where Mike Wise presented me with a check (less the ten percent commission) for $45,000. It was sure sweet to collect.

For the first time since I'd left Foote Cone & Belding and went into the Studio City office alone on January 1, 1968, three and a half years earlier, the Rosebrook family was solvent.

It had been over seven months since I'd left Joe Wizan's office at Warner Brothers with his instructions, "I want this for Steve McQueen." It had only been since April that Joe and I met Steve at his house and that famous question from the world's highest paid actor, "Doesn't he take notes?" Only weeks since Susan Hayward returned to Florida in a huff, and Ida came in, fighting her leftover Novocaine. Weeks to meet Lynn Stallmaster, Tiffany Bolling, Joe Don Baker, Bill McKinney. And yet to meet Robert Preston.

Only weeks since Sam threatened to tie that tin can to my ass and mail me home.

It was rare for the writer to be on location.

Perhaps Sam's tin can was simply on hold.

The cooperation of the Frontier Days Committee and the City of Prescott allowed Sam Peckinpah to direct the action of Curly Bonner's float and Steve McQueen and Robert Preston's interactions in the parade while the actual Fourth of July Parade was happening, which is one of the aspects that makes Junior Bonner *such an effective film.* Mike Siegel Collection.

The crowds who gathered along the streets of Prescott in 1971 to view the Frontier Days Fourth of July Parade had no idea that they would be part of a "cast of thousands" and make movie history that day.
All Parade Photos Courtesy Mike Siegel Collection except for middle photo (above)
Courtesy Jeff Slater Collection.

One of three major stunts that McQueen and Preston performed together was riding off together from the parade through a Prescott neighborhood, arguing over who should be in the saddle, before actually being "clotheslined" off their horse. Mike Siegel Collection.

The bond that occurred between Robert Preston and Steve McQueen, as well as the creative process between Sam Peckinpah, Jeb Rosebrook, the actors, and the crew led to the production of one of the finest scenes of the movie, if not the most important to all five principals involved in its creation. Rosebrook Family Collection.

Sam's relationship with his own father, including his habit of "cuffing" Sam's hat off when angry with him, was incorporated into the poignant scene between father and son at the Prescott train depot. Mike Siegel Collection.

The emotional scene with Preston and McQueen is held dear by many who commiserate with the father-son relationship between Ace and Junior. The scene was very personal for me, as it was for Sam and Steve, who even shed a tear during the action, a moment of vulnerability rarely ever shown by McQueen on screen. Mike Siegel Collection.

Robert Preston, in the Grand Entry of the Prescott Rodeo, had not acted in a feature film since 1963, and it had been ten years since he'd been astride a horse in How the West Was Won. Rosebrook Family Collection.

Peckinpah worked closely with each cast-member, no matter the size of their role, throughout the film. Well-known Western television actor Charles H. Gray (left) played the big-city dude Burt, who brought Barbara Leigh, as the charming bank teller, Charmagne, up to Prescott for the Fourth of July weekend. Mike Siegel Collection.

Choreographing scenes during rodeo week was one of the great challenges that Sam faced during the production of Junior Bonner. A crowd-pleasing free-for-all that many stock contractors no longer offer at modern rodeos is wild cow-milking, and Peckinpah, Preston, McQueen, and Joe Wizan had to carefully choreograph that scene to protect their stars from serious injury.
Mike Siegel Collection.

Two veteran actors, Preston and McQueen, bonded as closely as two professional actors could on a film, and their personal chemistry is evident in the spontaneity that occurs during the chaos of the wild cow-milking scene.
Rosebrook Family Collection.

At 41 and 53 respectively, McQueen and Preston approached their rodeo stunts in Junior Bonner, *including the wild cow-milking, as enthusiastic and able veterans of numerous Westerns and action films.* Mike Siegel Collection.

The friendship and bond that developed between Preston and McQueen on and off the set in Prescott during the summer of 1971 led to the dynamic chemistry witnessed on screen between "father" and "son." Mike Siegel Collection.

The two veteran leading men, Preston and McQueen, knew how to share a scene, and both knew they had succeeded in playing off their mutual admiration and love for each other—even in losing—during the wild cow-milking event. Close-up of Steve McQueen and Robert Preston in Arena, Courtesy Mike Siegel Collection/Steve McQueen and Robert Preston in Arena with Crew, Courtesy Jeff Slater Collection.

As a director, Peckinpah was at his best choreographing spontaneous action, and the wild cow-milking scene was a showcase for his talents in directing Preston and McQueen. Mike Siegel Collection.

Sam liked to put everyone "in the barrel" during the production of Junior Bonner, *and was constantly looking for a chance to test me. He knew of my background growing up at the Orme Ranch and high school rodeo, so he challenged me to participate in the wild cow-milking. I earned his respect that day, and also an honorary membership in the Stuntman's Association.*
First and Second Photo of Jeb Rosebrook in Arena, Courtesy Mike Siegel Collection/ Third Photo of Jeb Rosebrook, Courtesy Rosebrook Family Collection.

Dougal the Dog, trained by veteran Hollywood dog-trainer Frank
Weatherwax, was cast as Ace Bonner's man-biting, unfriendly dog. Dougal
almost stole the show when he got loose during the wild cow-milking event,
biting man and beast, and causing unrehearsed chaos wherever he went
in the arena. This prompted the announcer to yell out off-script, "And, will
someone get that damned dog!"

Dougal the Dog with Robert Preston, Courtesy Jeff Slater Collection/Dougal the Dog in
the Arena, Courtesy Mike Siegel Collection.

During the production of Junior Bonner, *Preston and McQueen spent a great deal of time together on set, sharing details of their characters' "business," including Junior rolling his own cigarettes.* Mike Siegel Collection.

*Sam Peckinpah's veteran property master, Bobby Visiglia, worked closely with
Steve McQueen throughout the production of* Junior Bonner.
Mike Siegel Collection.

Steve McQueen relaxing on the set of Junior Bonner *at the Yavapai County Fairgrounds in Prescott, Arizona, in the summer of 1971.* Jeff Slater Collection.

While Peckinpah was seven years younger than Robert Preston, they enjoyed a mutual respect on the set that led to Preston delivering a performance as "Ace" that revitalized his film career, a cinematic comeback that led to steady film and television work, including an Oscar nomination for Victor Victoria *(1982). He died at age 68 in 1987.* Mike Siegel Collection.

Peckinpah loved being behind the camera and working with his favorite cinematographer, Lucien Ballard, and his camera crew. Junior Bonner *was the fourth film the two had made together, plus Ballard had worked on Peckinpah's short-lived TV Western,* The Westerner *(NBC, 1960).* Mike Siegel Collection.

Sam Peckinpah cast Alex, a local Prescott cowboy, as a friend of Ace's in Junior
Bonner. *Alex had spent most of his life cowboying near Kingman and did not
know Preston was a famous Hollywood and Broadway actor.*
Mike Siegel Collection.

Robert Preston embraced his role of Ace Bonner with the same contagious enthusiasm and charisma that had brought him so much success and fame as the lead in Music Man *(1962) on Broadway and film.* Mike Siegel Collection.

As the crew prepared the lighting and set the camera, Peckinpah worked closely with McQueen and Preston to develop their on-film chemistry with each other and the extras, including two local girls cast to ride with Preston in the rodeo Grand Entry. Mike Siegel Collection.

Preston and McQueen worked with Casey Tibbs and the other wranglers and cowboys on the set before rehearsing with Peckinpah to assure their actions as rodeo cowboys were believable to the audience. Mike Siegel Collection.

McQueen and Preston enjoyed a quiet moment before Preston rode in the Grand Entry of the rodeo. Rosebrook Family Collection.

ACT TWO

Coming home to Prescott.

Junior Bonner was bringing me home.

Prescott entered my world of hometowns in 1945. We were a total of nine boys and girls from the Quarter Circle V Bar Ranch School, some thirty-odd miles to the east, on the dirt road known as the Black Canyon Highway. Our "parents" were Charles and Minna Orme, known to all of us as "Uncle Chick" and "Aunt Minna." Their oldest, Charlie, ran the ranch and at age twenty-six was in the process of taking over the school. His younger brother, Mort, was in the U.S. Marines in the South Pacific and the youngest, Katy, suffering from rheumatic fever, was a student at Stanford. The school began shortly after the Ormes purchased the 27,000-acre cattle ranch in 1928. The Yavapai County School was established for the Orme children and for those of Juan, whose family handled the ranch work. Soon enough, the small school began attracting asthmatic children from the East. Soon thereafter, a summer camp was established. In 1945, as an asthmatic fourth grader, I was the youngest in the class; the oldest was in the eighth grade. All of us were taught by Joan "Teach" Atterbury, a Massachusetts product and Wellesley graduate who had attended the school in the 1930s.

During the last week of June 1971, Sam arrived in his vintage red Porsche wearing the hat his friend Jason Robards had worn in *The Ballad of Cable Hogue* (1969).

For now, it was rehearsals. Or, possibly, the calm before the storm.

There was time for me to reflect on my personal pride of bringing so much to Prescott, not the least of which would be the dollars that were soon to flow from our presence to the businesses of the town, and the publicity generated for what some called "America's Hometown." It earned that title mostly for when the early morning sunlight lit the Yavapai County Courthouse, surrounded by trees and the grassy lawns, the Rough Rider statue, providing that feeling of comfort that this truly could be the hometown that should have been, and never was, painted by Norman Rockwell. Across from the courthouse was that long block known as Whiskey Row featuring the Palace Bar, which I included in so much of my screenplay. And at the edge of town, the fairgrounds, where lived The World's Oldest Rodeo begun as a "Cowboy Tournament" in 1888, where Tom Mix had once, as a local resident making silent film one-reelers, taken first prize in bull riding in 1913.

Yavapai College was home base for rehearsals. Sam sat in the main seat of the round table. Katy on one side of him and me on the other, scripts open, ready to take notes. "Ida" and "Bob," as we called them, since we'd very quickly became on first-name basis, were side-by-side. They had known one another since early film studio days as contract players at Paramount. Between them and Ben Johnson was Tiffany, young, blond, and eager, and on the far side of Ben was Steve, with a quiet onlooker, Joe Wizan.

One day during a break while washing up in the men's room, Sam told me how valuable his daily B-12 shots were to him. It showed. He had real energy. It also showed in his enthusiasm for the rewrites that, now in rehearsals, were final until before the camera. I admit now how little I knew about Sam Peckinpah, the writer/director. While aware of the talent shown in rewriting a standard B-Western, *Ride the High Country* (1962), and directing it into a classic, and equally aware of his writing talent shown in rewriting *The Wild Bunch* (1969) and *Cable Hogue* (1970), each molded into his vision, I did not know of the labors he put into building his writing skills via *Gunsmoke* (CBS, 1955-1975) and myriad other series in the television gold rush of half-hour Westerns. Then, in the final episode of *Broken Arrow* (ABC, 1956-1960), he'd had his first opportunity as a director.

Nor could I predict that within a decade, the brilliance would begin to fade into a forever haze of drugs and alcohol—and soon after, his life.

The rehearsal readings were very businesslike with minimal chitchat. With each reading, the dialogue became lean and leaner with little or no fat. Steve, half in jest, all in earnest, called me "Shakespeare" as he pared away his dialogue into his complete comfort zone. At one point he turned to Ben and then told all of us he had seen a screening of Peter Bogdonovich's adaptation of Larry McMurtry's novel *The Last Picture Show*. Presciently, Steve predicted that Ben was going to win an Academy Award for Best Supporting Actor. When Ben Johnson smiled, we knew, as he sensed, Steve was all admiration and truth.

We were a group totally in sync with one another and the script, with me, the first-time-produced film screenwriter, included. I would later learn it was rare for the writer to accompany the director on location. In fact, I think the director and actors prefer the writer not be around so they can alter lines and scenes as they wish. If the film turns out to be raved by the critics and audiences, the writer will get the credit. But if it heads for the basement of Rotten Tomatoes, the writer receives the large share of his or her blame, too.

I had settled into a room on the second floor of Prescott's most recent addition to the motel scene, The Prescottonian, with a handy café just at the foot of the parking lot. Sam had made certain my desk was equipped with a typewriter and plenty of paper. Tiffany was down the hall and, on the first floor, Bob and Ida. Sam and Steve rented their own private homes, and where Ben located himself, I have never been certain. Sam also had an office upstairs in the Palace—rooms that were once either a hotel or whorehouse or both!

In the reading, when we reached the dramatic scene between Bob and Ida on the back steps of the Palace where Ace Bonner is leaving for Australia and says his final good-bye to his estranged wife, "Then all we have is tonight," we were all emotionally moved, as were Bob and Ida. Emotion caused a pause of silence.

And Sam had tears in his eyes.

Tears welled in my eyes when Steve and Bob read the father/son scene at the railroad depot. And their final moment from father to son, "I've got us entered in the wild cow-milking." Marty Baum had been correct: the strength of an actor like Bob was bringing equal strength from Steve.

Each day the readings became tighter. I noted line changes and then typed them into script changes in my room. Betty Gumm, Joe's assistant, was organizing an office staff to enter changes into the script. Working with production secretary Dorothy Whitney,

Jim Pratt arrived to run the entire office as production manager. At sixty-one, Jim was the ultimate professional as production manager, having served in executive positions with virtually all the major studios, beginning his career as a carpenter in the 1920s.

But with cast and crew beginning to assemble, and Steve, more than rumored from splitting with Neile, *where is the media, I wondered.* Answer: there were none. It seems conceivable that part of Steve's business deal was no media interviews or photographs. After all the personal and professional distractions of *Le Mans,* Steve appeared well within his comfort zone—both with the script and with the town of Prescott.

"Let's look for road shots," Steve suggested to Sam and me one afternoon after rehearsals. Steve wanted to look at possible driving scenes and was inviting us to do the looking with him. So far, during the table readings, Sam and Steve were getting along well. After all, Steve had hosted Sam and Joe Wizan in Palm Springs the month before and all appeared in creative agreement on the script. It seemed whatever involvement Steve had—if any at all—in having Sam fired off *The Cincinnati Kid* was long forgotten. In fact, according to Sam Peckinpah biographer Garner Simmons, "Sam was fired by producer Martin Ransohoff a week into the production for allegedly filming an 'unauthorized' nude scene with Anne Margaret." (The truth was Ransohoff decided he did not agree with Sam's vision for the film.) Steve McQueen had no part in it. And in fact, given Sam's propensity for holding grudges, had McQueen had a hand in it, it would have prevented them from ever working together on either *Junior Bonner* or *The Getaway.*

"Get in the back," Steve told me as Sam joined him in the cab of Steve's 400-horsepower Chevrolet pickup. Steve chose the back way out of Prescott on the narrow two-lane twisting old U.S. 89 through the pine forests and out toward Yarnell and the downward spiral toward Wickenburg.

It turned out to be the wildest, scariest ride of my lifetime. It may have been a Chevy pickup truck, but Steve treated our drive as his own personal Formula One journey. The winding curves among the pines, held by late afternoon sunlight, were meant for Steve. But not necessarily for a white-knuckled passenger like me, hanging on for dear life.

After what seemed like forever, holding on as we took the curves at top speed, we reached the small town of Yarnell at the edge of high country looking toward one long spiral down to the desert. Thankfully, we turned around.

Was this wild ride *mano y mano* from Sam to Steve? Not to mention Shakespeare holding on for his life in the bed of the Chevy.

I believe Steve was letting Sam and me know he was Steve McQueen. In charge.

It was a moment in time not lost on Sam Peckinpah.

***

Next came the arrivals of Lucien Ballard and Lynn Stallmaster.

Lucien, Sam's cinematographer on *Ride the High Country*, *The Wild Bunch*, and *Cable Hogue* was Sam's most valuable asset behind the Panavision camera. Lynn was in town to cast extras and smaller roles. To assist him, I recommended William S. "Buck" Hart, Jr., West Virginia native, an English teacher, kazoo player, full-time— in mind and action—thespian, part-time cowboy from my alma mater, the nearby Orme School. Buck was interviewed by Lynn for the sole task of hiring locals. He was hired, and the two of them immediately hit it off.

Lucien was then sixty-three years old. Part Cherokee and a native Oklahoman, he had been educated at the University of Oklahoma and the University of Pennsylvania before striking out for travel in China and winding up in Hollywood on his return. He began his career at Paramount in 1929. At just twenty-one years old, he was already recognized as one with an eye with the camera. His career included marriage to (and divorce from) movie star Merle Oberon, work with Howard Hughes on the infamous Jane Russell picture *The Outlaw* (1943), and Henry Hathaway on *Prince Valiant* (1954), *Sons of Katie Elder* (1965), *Nevada Smith*, and *True Grit* (1969) among many, prior to providing the visual eye to Sam on *Ride the High Country* (1962).

Tall and with a striking lionesque presence, Lucien was in command of his chosen crew of cameramen, gaffers, and grips—total command.

Buck Hart, then in his forties, was tall, angular and with a craggy face that once met, was easily remembered. His dream of becoming a real cowboy had come true fifteen years earlier when he came west from his native West Virginia home with wife, Jan, and two boys, Doug and Chris, to teach English and Drama at the Orme School and cattle ranch. Perhaps it was in the Navy during World War II (he could never forget being on the ground for the Battle of Peleliu) that he took up the kazoo. His signature song was "Tangerine" (w. Victor Schertzinger and Johnny Mercer). If Buck had been a full-time actor, there would never be a scene he would not steal.

Then came Frank Kowalski. Also in his forties, Frank was half-Polish and half-Mexican. He was the son of a film editor with family roots traced back to the border town of Brownsville, Texas. Following recent work as an assistant director on the Vic Morrow television series *Combat!* (ABC, 1962-1967), he had begun working with Sam as a dialogue director on *The Wild Bunch*. I will learn Frank's creativity had no bounds for story content. He recently had penned his own Western, filmed in Mexico with James Garner, and co-written with Vic Morrow, *A Man Called Sledge* (1970). Unlike Sam, Frank had a Hollywood pedigree, with his brother, Bernie, becoming a successful director in television. The Kowalski brothers' father had been a film editor for director Michael Curtiz during Curtiz's most creative years with Warner Brothers.

I heard that Sam had a longtime impatience with Frank in fulfilling what Sam felt was Frank's creative potential. So, when Frank came to Sam announcing his fulfillment on *Sledge*, Sam, as legend would have it, complimented him by knocking his front teeth out— as if to say "What took you so long?"—and yet, here was Frank. For Sam, Frank was indispensable as a man of many talents. Each their own man, they were on good terms now, as Frank was working on a story for Sam to write and direct, *Bring Me the Head of Alfredo Garcia* (1974). Frank was hired initially as a dialogue director.

From the documentary, *Rodeo* with Tornado the bull, directed by Carrol Ballard, Joe chose Ballard, thirty-four, for second unit director. Based on what I had seen, the ride "Freckles" Brown had made on Tornado was the true-life counterpart of Junior's challenge to ride Sunshine. In their Palm Springs meeting, Joe was certain Sam and Carrol were "going to be instrumental together." He added that Sam will realize the world of "today's rodeo" in Carrol's documentary and "you ought to be able to really pick his brains."

Based on Carrol's documentary, he seemed like an ideal choice to me, but he had to be on the same wavelength as Sam Peckinpah.

***

The production meeting: Jim Pratt needed a break in the budget. It would be extremely expensive to film the day rodeo, and bull-riding-at-night rodeo, after the Palace Bar and a hellacious fight before going out to film a single nighttime bull ride. Or, creatively, where will the drama be if we film the entire rodeo ending with Junior riding Sunshine and then go to the Palace for Charmagne and Junior? Or what if we took the entire crew out just to film the night show's bull riding? The drama is with Sunshine. Two changes: we simply have our rodeo announcer tell the crowd they will take a break, similar to halftime in football, go down to the Palace, where we will have the truly all-hell-breaking-loose fight, then return to the rodeo for the final afternoon events, the last of which is Junior and Sunshine.

I wonder how rodeo purists will handle such a move. In my mind, there had never been a professional rodeo where the audience took a break, went off to drink and dance, then return to the remainder of the rodeo—all in one afternoon!

Bottom line: to stay on budget, this is the way it will be done.

About the planned Palace Bar fight: My initial screenplay placed emphasis on Junior and Charmagne. Two people meet, the music plays, they dance, and a relationship—call it a "Woodstock" getting together, if you will—ensues. When the sun comes up tomorrow, Charmagne heads back to Phoenix in her VW bug while Junior, in his well-worn Cadillac, ornament to better days, heads down the road to his next rodeo.

Sam felt that was not enough to sustain audience interest. He had me create a moment interrupting Junior and Charmagne with the eruption of a fight that soon took in everyone, leaving Junior and Charmagne to their privacy. Not only that, but he cast longtime actor and stuntman Charles Gray to be Charmagne's main squeeze, which precipitates the brawl that spread like a wildfire throughout the Palace.

Charles Gray is one of those actors I wished I had known better and stayed in touch with over the years. At age fifty, Charles was an actor whose face, but not his name, was recognizable for years as a guest on television series and for a permanent five-year part as Clay Forrester on *Rawhide* (CBS, 1959-1965). Charles was a true professional.

One more important piece of casting was Dougal the dog. Trained by the Weatherwax family, there will be a good Dougal with false teeth when he growled, and a bad Dougal who will bite you in the ass. And there will be no lack of action for the dog Dougal of my creation. Make no doubt about it, he would bite.

For music, I had written in specific songs for the Palace segment. During this period of rehearsals and pre-production we had a chance to meet the band playing the Palace. Leader of the band was Bob Cox. His lead singer, a smooth Country crooner, was Rod Hart. During the dance scenes I had written in specific songs, "Proud Mary" (w. John Fogerty) by Creedence Clearwater Revival and Merle Haggard's "Today I Started Loving You Again." Additionally, I inserted a Stan Jones song that Rex Allen had a hit with in 1951, "Cowpoke." I'd remembered it from years before as a student at Orme School, and penned it into the script to be sung by a rodeo stock-hand while feeding the horses. Music was important to me when I was writing the screenplay. Especially meaningful were Judy Collins's version of Ian Tyson's "Someday Soon" and the empathy for coming home with John Denver's "Take Me Home, Country Roads" (w. Bill Danoff, Taffy Nivert, and John Denver).

I assumed from the magnificent Jerry Fielding score for *The Wild Bunch* and the forthcoming *Straw Dogs* that he would score *Junior Bonner*. Furthermore, there was a rumor that Buck Owens would play the Palace for our dancing and fight sequence, yet in the few remaining days of rehearsals and pre-production, there was more than a rumor that Buck and his Buckaroos of Bakersfield were proving too expensive for Jim Pratt's budget and, like a movie story fairy tale, Rod Hart and Bob Cox delivered two songs to the producers, after reading the script. The songs, titled "Arizona Morning" and "Rodeo Man," were given to Sam, passed up the chain of command, and accepted. (Many years later, I was made aware that Bob Cox never understood why he was not credited in the lyrics and music of either song, but Universal Songs published both songs registered with BMI, both lyrics and music, credited exclusively to Rod Hart.)

As the full film crew arrived, I was getting to know them and, as the writer on location, taken in as one of them and treated with equal respect. I had only been on a set once and that was when Howard Christie took me on the set of *The Virginian* to meet the actors on the backlot at Universal. I quickly learned that I was in the major leagues of film.

Sam's prop man, soon enough to prove indispensable, was Bobby Visciglia, the U.S. Navy veteran who never was broke because extra dollars were always tucked away in his shoe. We soon learned as well that Bobby was there to be certain any need of Sam's was taken care of, pronto. A true professional at his job, a man of humor and expansive personality, Bobby and his prop truck assisted not just the film, but the needs of all, including our advertising tie-ins with Coca-Cola, Miller Beer, and Wild Turkey Bourbon.

Art Director Ted Haworth, fifty-four, had worked with Joe Wizan and Sidney Pollock in Utah on *Jeremiah Johnson*. The more I would get to know Ted, the more I came to appreciate him as an artist and as a quiet, modest professional and warm human being. I did not know his credits included an Academy Award in 1957 for *Sayonara*, *The Longest Day*, *Strangers on a Train*, *Invasion of the Body Snatchers*, and *Some Like it Hot*—and perhaps the greatest compliment to me, that my writing put me in a league with Paddy Chayefsky, one of my writing heroes.

While the town embraced us as newcomers, there was a hard element of locals who felt we Hollywood types were soft and here to "play cowboy." Their stares were obvious when we gathered at night for drinks at the Palace or at Matt's Saloon, a honky-tonk next door that was owned by Matt Butitta.

It came as no surprise when a well-known, good-sized local cow-boy decided to see how real Ben was. It began inside the Palace when the local had started egging Ben on for a fight, and continued outside. Ben, who was a gentle soul, was not taking the bait. The more Ben ignored the cowboy, the angrier and more aggressive he became. Finally, enough was enough. Ben turned around.

"Listen here," Ben said. "If you say one more word, I'll knock the shit out of you."

At that the cowboy smiled and held out his hand.

"You are just the man I thought you was," he said as he took Ben's hand and shook it. There might be Steve McQueen in Prescott, but to the working ranch cowboys, the real star was Ben Johnson.

To Casey, Ben, and Ross Dollarhide, there was one former rodeo comrade they respected above all—Chuck Sheppard. At fifty-five, Chuck, a native Arizonan, had retired from rodeo to train and breed thoroughbreds at the nearby Keickhefer K-4 Ranches. When inducted into the Pro Rodeo Hall of Fame, the former world cham-pion team roper was described as "the toughest four-event man there ever was." A further description was "a rider of tough horses and roper of wild cattle."

When Chuck invited Ben, Casey, and Ross to a barbecue, I was invited to join them. These were the real men of their times, who came up in an era when professional rodeo cowboys were still con-sidered by some—like Casey's father, who raised horses along the Cheyenne River in South Dakota—to be no more than carnival performers. Chuck was once a part of the Cooper Brothers/Gene Autry Rodeo that, each year, played Pittsburgh, Boston, and New York's Madison Square Garden, spending weeks in each city, includ-ing nearly a month in Manhattan before moving on to Boston. Many, like Casey and Montana's Bud Linderman, had deserved reputations as rounders and when in New York, as "enemies" of the NYPD, Chuck earned his way quietly and successfully, always sending earnings home.

Casey made sure Chuck had a speaking part in the film.

(Something else I took away from that evening: cooking steaks over a wood fire is far superior to grilling with charcoal or gas.)

Locations were now all locked in. The former grand 1927 Has-
syampa Hotel, now a HUD retirement apartment house, will be
the hospital where Ace Bonner is treated after his pickup wreck on
Cherry Creek Road. A Victorian-style home, dating back to past
decades, has been chosen for Elvira's home and gift shop. The dance
hall/saloon/restaurant Reata Pass, outside of Prescott in the town
of Humboldt, will be the business site of Curly Bonner's real estate
project; a gas station not far away, will be where Junior and his old
Cadillac stop for gas and an oil check (40 weight). Also outside of
Prescott, is a lonely strip of land on which an aged, small, abandoned
wooden home stands—a more-than-perfect choice for demolition
by a bulldozer to make way for Curly's real estate retirement homes.
The Palace was as is. The Santa Fe railroad depot was as is. Sam
chose the opposite side of Prescott and the highway there, and not
Steve's wild ride section of old U.S. 89 on the other side of town.
Granite Dells, a beautiful landscape of unique rock formations and
a lake is chosen for an opening sequence; unfortunately, its water
level is lower than usual but it's still visually scenic. Downtown and
the Courthouse Plaza are as they are. And Ted Haworth and his
crew are at work on a long, sweeping tractor-pulled float that Curly
will enter in the parade.

One member of the cast had yet to be chosen: Sunshine the Bull.

In my original screenplay, working with Joe Wizan, the initial
scene did not introduce Junior but his father, Ace, and his dog, Dougal, as bulldozers move in to demolish the old Bonner homestead.

For Sam, this action, the destruction of the family homestead,
could come later. He wanted the action of man-against-animal to
open the film, as Junior attempts the eight-second ride on a bull
named Sunshine. Junior does not make the eight seconds. He is
thrown off, nearly trampled, and badly hurt. Dramatically, this
played into Junior's need to face the challenge of riding Sunshine
again, and, importantly, to do it in front of his hometown folks. The
new opening provided the introduction of Junior's main rival, Red
Terwiliger, played by Bill McKinney. It also established Junior as a
veteran rodeo hand, and judging by the character of his old Cadillac
convertible, whose best years were behind him. The theme of their

rivalry also stood as a storyline throughout the script, including moments with Charmagne in the Palace.

Now established as one of the world's top film directors with a flair for violence for which, other than Sergio Leone, he had no equal, Sam had found a unique way to open a film, to grab and bring the audience immediately into the story he was about to tell. It happened in *The Wild Bunch* as children found delight and cruel fascination watching ants and a scorpion fight one another for survival while being burned alive. It happened as well in the opening of *The Ballad of Cable Hogue* as a Gila monster, blown away, explodes before our eyes.

So now an angry, if not terrifying, Brahma bull will open *Junior Bonner*.

One night at the rodeo grounds, several Brahma bulls were auditioned. With the chutes manned by stunt extras, who also rodeoed professionally, and with Sam giving the orders, three cameras were ready to film the audition. These huge bulls would not be ridden but will be challenged by a rodeo clown, with his barrel as his safe haven.

Sam stationed himself close by the chutes, where the bulls would be released; none of the bulls were to be released from their chutes until his command.

There are several versions of what happened that night. One was an impatient Sam speaking loudly and disparagingly, cursing out a local cowboy for a mistake made at the chutes—which one should never do in the company of real cowboys. It could be said, or legend may have it, that professional bull rider and stuntman Frank Kelly did take offense to Sam's use of language and where it was directed.

Quite suddenly, a chute was left open while the director and others' attention were on a current bull and clown in the area.

Through the open chute charged a raging black bull.

WHAT THE FUCK?!

The bull charged past the stunned clown, who dove down into his barrel. The bull kept going and going and going, heading for the fence across the area and the camera crew operating a $20,000 Panavision camera.

The crew scattered. The bull collided with the fence and the $20,000 camera, which was destroyed.

"Who left the fucking gate open?" demanded our director.

"Maybe it was you," murmured a cowboy out of earshot of Sam.

No one spoke up to answer the question.

Nevertheless, a bull was chosen.

And the following night, Bill Pierce's son, an Arizona State high school rodeo champion, did ride that bull for the opening sequence of the film. That, too, was nearly a disaster. In the script, for his hopeful eight-second ride, Junior is to have his hand entangled while gripping the rope, called being "hung up," in rodeo terms. Only he was not faking it, he really was hung up. This time was more fortunate than the previous night. He managed to extricate himself from the rope and make a strong stunt fall to the ground.

But it made for damn good film.

It happened that afternoon, two days before cameras rolled for the parade. I walked down Whiskey Row with Tiffany Bolling. She was relaxed, knowing she had a week now before she had to step before the camera.

The scene, meeting Junior, had been reworked. Sam now wanted Charmagne to be on the arm of Charles Gray, a wealthy follower of rodeo, and thus meet Junior beside his trailer before the rodeo events begin. This is where Sam's true sense of the story kicked in: why wait for Junior to meet Charmagne? Why have her just another young woman driving up to Prescott in a VW Bug? Why not put her on the arm of this rich guy?

This, to Sam, will be the cause for the major fight scene he envisioned for the Palace—all part of the rewriting which had to do with having a "half-time" break in the rodeo, where everyone headed for the Palace.

Another lesson learned—that filmmaking is so often a collaboration of the trio of writer, director, and actor.

Except, after this day walking down Whiskey Row, I will never see Tiffany Bolling again.

"She left for a female operation in L.A.," I was told. "She'd be a medical insurance risk if she came back," I heard.

Shortly thereafter, Barbara Leigh arrived in a near-brand new Mercedes with her young son in tow. They were moving in, just down the hall from me.

I recalled Steve glancing out the window as she crossed the studio parking lot after she read for the part of Charmagne. With an impending divorce, he'd assured himself of summer companionship. Barbara was not only a high-fashion beauty model, perfect for the part of being the mistress type on the arm of wealthy Charles Gray, but what Steve might not have known (and certainly I did not) was that Barbara was also the girlfriend of president of MGM James T. Aubrey, known as the "Smiling Cobra" for his business acumen, as well as to the King himself, Elvis Presley. Nor did any of us know or should know was that her 1971 250 C Mercedes was a personal gift from the King.

There is no doubt that Barbara, as the role was now rewritten from my original vision for Charmagne, was perfect casting for the "new" Charmagne. Yet, I always felt badly for Tiffany. She had the looks, the style, and the acting ability for how I saw as the then-Charmagne. I never saw Tiffany again, nor did I know the truth of her departure or "female" medical treatment. I heard through others she was very bitter about what happened to what was to be the biggest break in her young career. From that point on, Tiffany's main roles were in B-films, with an emphasis on her looks and sexuality. Hollywood sure can be a bitch.

And I learned that Barbara did not arrive by happenstance as Tiffany was leaving. Barbara had already been dating Steve in California. A relationship had been set in motion before she got to Prescott.

I found Barbara Leigh fun to be around, a wonderful personality with no pretentions about her acting ability. What turned out to be most important was that the Steve/Barbara relationship in real-time Prescott translated beautifully to film.

Sam also had those to share his life at his rental home in Prescott. I saw Mary Murphy only at Sam's, but perhaps she was living elsewhere. Also on hand for the director was a major love in his life: Begonia Palacios, a former flamenco dancer whom Sam had cast in *Major Dundee*. This is where their longtime love affair began (they actually married three times), with loyal-and-in-love Katy Haber in between, and sometimes-for-real Joie Gould in the mix.

Long divorced from college sweetheart Marie Selland, Sam brought his daughter, Sharon, and son, Matthew, to Prescott to be a part of the film, and perhaps Kristen and Melissa were also with their dad. Also within the Peckinpah group was Gary Weiss, whom we came to know as "Gary Good Guy," who was there to film a documentary on the making of the movie.

On the day before filming, I met Joe Don Baker and Bill McKinney downstairs in Joe Don's room at the Prescottonian. I had not really connected with them since the readings at the studio. Joe Don asked if I wanted a joint and, strictly a Marlboro man, I declined. These, to me, were good guys. Although my age and older, both had worked hard at their acting craft and careers and, being Southern-born—Texas and Tennessee, respectively—they clearly were not to be trifled with.

Dub Taylor arrived in his red Toyota Landcruiser and took his place at the Prescottonian. Dub brought with him his endearing trademark Georgia accent. Don "Red" Barry was now here as well. I found the Republic Pictures hero of my boyhood reclusive, quiet, yet not without ego. Soon enough, when announced to the rodeo crowd, he was a top box-office draw in 1944.

On the night before filming, we all attended the rodeo where Casey Tibbs, who gave himself the claim as "Possibly America's Most Beloved Cowboy," had been named Grand Marshall for the Frontier Days parade. Casey chose to be a part of the saddle bronc competition. His introduction provided the crowd with a rodeo pedigree that placed him as the greatest saddle and bareback bronc-rider of all time.

Casey came out of the chute giving the crowd a show of greatness—for almost ten seconds. He leaned way back, spurs raking the shoulders of his bronc, and then took a sudden (perhaps planned?) fall to the ground. And there he lay. Unmoving. Is it possible serious injury has befallen Possibly America's Most Beloved Cowboy? The ambulance arrived. Casey was carried on a stretcher into the waiting ambulance. Away he went.

At a production meeting later that evening, I mentioned my concern about Casey to Sam. He had neither concern nor interest in Casey.

"He's man enough," he said. The meeting continued.

Five cameras would cover the parade from every street angle, including Curly's float, where Junior would climb aboard, looking for his dad, Ace. I was proud of my line, "He's up there, between the Indians and the flag." Close-up scenes featuring Ida and Bob, and Steve and Bob, would be filmed later. But for now, we had only one chance of filming the real-time parade.

A word of caution went out to all. "An airplane flew most of you over here. Fuck up and you're on the bus [to home]." A stern warning from Sam Peckinpah

The Sam I was growing to know was not to me a man of popular music. Yet one song he liked to hear on the jukebox at the Palace or Matt's seemed to me, real or imagined, a personal hymn to the life of all of us in our summer ahead: Lynn Anderson's "(I Never Promised You A) Rose Garden" (w. Joe South).

The parade. Cameras roll!

Our son, Stuart, was attending the nearby Orme Ranch Summer Camp, where once I had been a summer ranch hand and, the following year, a camp counselor. The Orme summer campers annually attended the parade, riding from the ranch to Prescott in the back of an open stakebed truck. Many of the campers would also be participants in the parade. Older campers rode two-by-two in drill team formation, while younger campers rode in a red and white covered wagon with the Quarter Circle V Bar Ranch emblazoned on the side. I had a chance to meet with Stuart before the parade. He was not only excited to be with fellow campers in Prescott but proud of his dad, who had created the story for the about-to-be-filmed parade. Dorothy and Katherine were to arrive for a visit the following week.

Fourth of July parades, as we all know, are very much a part of our national pride and fabric. Prescott and its iconic, historic town plaza are sewn into that fabric. As five cameras rolled, bands marched and played, clowns and Shriners paraded, the legendary Bill Williams Mountain Men rode horseback, Grand Marshall Casey Tibbs doffed his hat (showing no effects of his horse fall), and more bands played. There were the Orme campers, and young campers from nearby Friendly Pines Camp in a horse-driven stagecoach and, sure, enough, there came Curly Bonner's real estate Reata Rancheros float, with hot pants "Dudettes" riding in back, watched over by Curly's wife, Ruth (Mary Murphy), and Joe Don offering the crowd the gifts of hard candy.

This was to be Steve's first scene in the film. He must come on foot to the float in the midst of the actual parade. Emotions from scenes yet to be filmed will be played out between Joe Don ("I'm gonna whip your ass, Junior." Junior smiles, "Well, it won't be the first time, Curly.") and Steve and a pissed-off Ruth, who coldly calls Steve only "JR."

(Bill Pierce brought Steve to the scene within the parade on Bill's own motorcycle. "I wanted him to drive, but he insisted I drive," recalls Pierce. "That was a trip. We stopped and smoked several cigarettes while we waited." When it was time, Steve McQueen, to the surprise of parade-goers, broke through the crowd, bound for the float.)

Ace Bonner, as Joe Don tells brother Junior, is riding up ahead, "between the Indians and the flag." Soon after, Junior catches up with his dad, joins him, riding double, and off they went turning a corner, in a scene to be later continued, as a cluster of antique automobiles pounded their horns, startling Ace's horses and nearly dumping Ace and Junior to the street.

To Sam and his camera commander-in-chief Lucien Ballard it was more than just parade shots but closer shots of the people themselves, revealing a true portrait of an American Fourth of July (in reality a nation fractured by the Vietnam War) as the parade made its way around the Courthouse Plaza.

I thought of Stuart seeing through his eight-year-old eyes the cameras filming a moment in time created for the movie screen by his dad; and how this all happened to a dad who left advertising two and a half years ago for an office in Studio City to which he journeyed each day, spending time with his own father's 1948 Royal portable typewriter, with thoughts and words and characters, five and a half days a week.

Almost as it had begun, the parade was over.

And that afternoon, began the first real scene in the film.

***

Junior is paying his entry fee to enter the rodeo. The filming moves to the fairgrounds and the real rodeo. Sam, I began to understand, would cast real Yavapai County folks in this film. So it was that he cast Bill Pierce as the local rodeo official who took the entry money and drew the draws for broncs and bulls. The scene was changed from my original to accommodate the real location behind the rodeo grounds and grandstands. Bill was also a major mover, not only for bringing the film to Prescott, but as chairman of the Prescott Jaycees Frontier Days Rodeo Committee. The scene would play off the film's opening, when Junior gets hung up on the bull called Sunshine, gets thrown, and leaves a bruised and banged-up bull rider. He has a moment with his longtime rival Red Terwiliger, which ends with "See you in Prescott, JR."

Junior is determined to draw Sunshine and this time, ride the bull in front of his hometown folks. In the film story, this is a tricky moment, tricky because there is no way to write the event as fixed so Junior will draw Sunshine again. Later in the filming, there will come a strong scene, which will precede in story sequence, the entry drawing, when Junior tells Buck Roan (Ben Johnson), the stock contractor, he needs to ride Sunshine because "it's my hometown." Junior tells Buck that it's not the money. "Money's nobody's favor," Junior tells him.

The irony of the story occurs when they draw for the bulls. Junior's draw gives him a second chance to ride Sunshine. For Red Terwiliger and the other contestants, it is no less a consensus that Junior has found a second opportunity to get his ass thrown into the dirt once again.

It was the first time, other than two moments in the parade since Howard Christie took me to the set of *The Virginian* two years before, that I actually got to see an entire scene filmed that I created. Joe Wizan stood beside me. "I want this for Steve McQueen," he had told me. Before our eyes it was happening.

This was day one...forty-seven more to go.

On to the rodeo the next day.

Dust, calves, and steers at one end of the arena, bucking horses and bulls corralled behind the chutes. The afternoon rodeo is in full swing and I am with Frank Kowalski and his part of Caroll

Ballard's second unit camera team. In my years growing up on the Orme Ranch I had often been a part of roundup with cattle and branding but never the fast pace that is rodeo: going from one event to the next, moving calves and steers into position for calf roping, steer wrestling, and team roping, as well as the bucking horses and bulls for their events. In my virgin rodeo excitement, I quickly moved here and there, shouting out excited thoughts for camera shots as we went along the fences, peering right into the faces and closer to the eyes of our animals. All the while, behind us, there were ropers, steer wrestlers, headers, and heelers for team roping, all going about their events. (Carroll Ballard and his unit were at the bucking and bull chutes.) I experienced a real rush; I continually felt I was finding great shots as an active part of the creative team.

During the company dinner at Yavapai College that evening, a very different tone and reaction quickly overcame the evening. I was called over to Sam's table, where Frank and Lucien sat with him. Only Sam spoke.

"Frank tells me you were a pain in the ass out there today," he began. "You were always in the goddamn way," he continued. And continued from there. This virgin rodeo camera guy was shocked and hurt. I said I thought I was of help to Frank. Frank said nothing. I stood to the silence.

Then they all laughed. They had put me on. But half in jest, all in earnest?

Awkwardly, I returned to my dinner.

I had been baptized in what was aptly named in the Peckinpah universe as "You're in the barrel."

The next day, while Sam, Lucien, and the full crew went out to film the demolition of Ace's old family homestead, my assignment was to spend time with Casey, Ben, and Ross Dollarhide to make sure real rodeo cowboy dialogue was included in the rodeo scenes. I may be thirty-five years old but I am just a wet-behind-the-ears kid with this trio of giants in their world. We gathered in Casey's room, and Ben takes time to break into this story of finding this book in a men's room in New Orleans. "This, here, book, damned if it wasn't called *Saturday*. How about that?" How did Ben know about my novel? Like Sam, Frank, and Lucien, Casey and Ross were just as serious as Ben, before they broke out in laughter. I laughed with them. The meeting went on. I passed another test.

Ben added an important reminder. My straw cowboy hat (I had borrowed from Buck Hart) was on the bed beside where I was seated. "Cowboy never leaves his hat on the bed," Ben told me. Where this axiom came from I, do not know. But it came from Ben, and agreement from Casey and Ross sealed Ben's pronouncement. For forty-five years, I have never put a hat on the bed.

Before the meeting broke up, Ben added some early history of Possibly America's Most Beloved Cowboy. He recalled the Cheyenne Frontier Days and a very young Casey Tibbs. "Here comes this skinny kid wanting to enter. Hell, he had to have a letter from his mother for him to enter."

The beginning of the legend.

That was to be the last day I spent any time in my room rewriting.

"Where the hell have you been?" Sam wanted to know. I told him where I was assigned to rewrite, in my room.

"From now on, I want you by my side."

There are doubtless numerous scenes in Peckinpah films that, for a moment, punctuate the man's brilliance. And genius. The gravel quarry scene, not scripted, is one of brilliance. And, as he'd commanded, I was by his side.

The heat of the July day was intense. Not far from where Sam's bulldozers would demolish the Ace Bonner homestead, he had located a working gravel quarry. The location was intently active with clouds of swirling thick dust, grinding machinery, and huge earth-movers.

In the story, Junior has arrived back in Prescott. He has set about to find his father, Ace Bonner, a one-time rodeo champion—"a champion of his time," as I described him. Junior goes first to the old homestead. There is no Ace. Ted Haworth had done a production design of the interior which evoked so much of what the audience will need to know about our Ace: the old rodeo photographs now covered with dust, license plates of other years and states illustrative of a man who never could settle down. An 8 x 10 photograph of Ace Bonner, the man in younger days.

Leaving the old home behind, Junior is on his way out when he comes face-to-face with the gravel quarry. He and his Cadillac must travel through the quarry to get out. Here, the combination of Sam and Lucien Ballard combine to create a near-abstract painting of the quarry's grinding machinery to make a filmic statement for Junior and all: This is not the West of Old. This is the beginning of the New West, the New Frontier—real estate. The emphatic punctuation arrives when Junior and his old Cadillac convertible come up against the monster earth-mover, blocking his way, blade raised menacingly as if prepared for battle. And refusing for the moment to retreat.

There is no blood to be spilled as in *The Wild Bunch* or *Ride the High Country*, no farewell to the West as Jason Robards as Cable Hogue is struck down by an automobile in *The Ballad of Cable Hogue*. This is man and machinery carving the way for a New West to be more than real estate-speculation, but people and homes, schools, condominiums, and paved roads leading to shopping centers and strip malls.

Junior shouts over the noise, through the dust, to a quarry worker that he is looking for Ace Bonner.

"Never heard of him," is the shouted reply.

Vanishing Ace. Vanishing West. A scene of brilliance played as such by Steve, who had looked for his own real father. A scene of brilliance as if the ghost of Sam's beloved central California ranch-land then being sold by his own mother for a housing development.

Sam was not finished with the gravel pit. But he had not planned on returning.

The rains came. And the gravel pit returned to him.

In the summer months, thunderstorms grow out of the nearby Bradshaw Mountains, once home to the Apaches and the gold-seekers who found their fortune in 1863. The temperature briefly plummets, hail often accompanies the storm and, within the hour, the storm has passed.

What Sam did not need for filming close-ups in the arena was mud.

Once again, enter Bill Pierce, fast becoming indispensable. "It started raining," Pierce recalled, "and all Sam's scheduled close-ups were in the mud and there was no 'dust.' In order to keep his filming schedule, Sam had to have dust.

"I had the tractors plow, but to no avail to get down [beneath the mud] to the dust. I called my friend that owned the gravel pit we used [also] for Ace's house and told Oakie I needed dust. He told me to go to hell, but I kept on and three semis loaded with dust came rolling into the arena. Oakie was driving the first truck and he asked where I wanted it. Sam was sitting in his director's chair under an umbrella and I told Oakie to dump it as close as he could to Sam but don't 'drown him.' I thought Sam was going to have a fit getting dirty, but we spread the dust and Sam continued shooting.

"Sam later came over laughing and said, 'I have made films all over the world and asked for a lot of things but never asked for dust and got it.'

"My reply was, 'You've never been to Prescott before.'"

The next real jolt on the set was Sam firing another crew member. Peckinpah was legendary for sending people home, and I was learning quickly that when Sam fired someone, it happened suddenly and without warning. Our highly gifted second unit director, Carroll Ballard, hired because of his brilliant work on *Rodeo* when Freckles Brown rode Tornado, was abruptly fired and vanished.

I had barely met him. Carroll Ballard was here, then quickly, he was gone. What happened? Apparently, the second unit film crew, well-seasoned IATSE veterans had complained to Lucien Ballard that Carroll seemed, so far, incapable of being a team player in the way he used them. Lucien passed this on to Sam.

Easy for me to figure. Carroll Ballard's camera affinity in *Rodeo* was primarily with the animals, particularly Tornado, as the bull related to Freckles. A UCLA film school graduate and a classmate of Francis Ford Coppola, Carroll was seen by Joe Wizan and ABC Pictures as perfect for the Sunshine and rodeo part of the script. Carroll was a purist as a documentary filmmaker. I am sure he never thought he needed more than himself as his own crew. He had never, to my knowledge, been involved in a major film with a crew of film veterans under his command. Visually, the shots were already filmed and edited in his own mind.

Sam heard the complaints. It was easy to tie the can to his ass and mail him home. What he did not need was some young (Ballard was my age) strong-willed documentary filmmaker to deal with on a daily basis for the next forty-plus days.

Carroll was with us for such a short time that *Junior Bonner* is not listed among his IMDb credits.

Over a drink and friendship, Sam appointed Frank Kowalski as second unit director.

Although we saw little of him, there was also Gary "Good Guy" Weiss here and there filming his behind-the-scenes making-of-a-movie documentary. Sam could have also thought, in firing Carroll Ballard, he had Gary as a backup.

Soon enough, Steve and Barbara would make their debut scene together at the rodeo grounds. While I was always with Sam, my time with Steve was only in the company of Sam. Barbara's intimate time with Steve, which began the evening after reading for the part of Charmagne, continued in real life as if Junior and Charmagne were meant for far more than a one-night movie-story stand. As Barbara, with Marshall Terrill (ironically, Steve's biographer, as well), wrote in her autobiography, *The King, McQueen and the Love Machine: My Secret Hollywood Life with Elvis Presley, Steve McQueen and the Smiling Cobra*: "In fact our backgrounds were almost identical. Both of us had lived in foster homes and children's homes. We had been deserted by our fathers at an early age. Both of us had mothers who were not equipped to raise us, mothers who were free spirits and had too many relationships with men throughout their lives."

Barbara added, as if for the punctuation of a summer in Prescott with the highest-paid actor in the world who had recently made the decision to leave his wife of many years, "There was a longing in his ice blue gaze, a slight sadness. We fit perfectly as lovers."

She recalled Steve called to tell her the part of Charmagne was hers. He told her to call Joe Wizan, who said only that Tiffany Bolling got sick.

Barbara recalled: "And there it was in the snap of a finger, I was to be Steve McQueen's leading lady. Not only did I get the leading man, but I got the part, too! Who says you can't have it all?

"[Sam] seemed nice enough. However, I think that Steve pulled some major strings to get me the part because of the vibes I was getting from Sam. I found out later I wasn't even Sam's second choice."

To the actor who had wanted to put the disaster of *Le Mans* behind him, Prescott seemed the perfect solution. He had brought with him two motocross bikes. "I was able to get a guy to let him into an old track that had been closed," Bill Pierce remembers. "He came just about every evening and got my fifteen-year-old son and they rode the track. It was awesome to watch Steve ride."

As author Marshall Terrill succinctly put it in his biography, *Steve McQueen, the Life and Legend of a Hollywood Icon*: "Turning forty had not been an easy milestone for Steve McQueen. When he looked in the mirror, he saw a middle-aged man staring back. His 'Live Now, Pay Later' attitude had finally caught up with him, and he was reeling.

"By the start of 1971, Steve McQueen had experienced the 'star trip' of booze, drugs, indiscriminate sex and an impending divorce."

According to Terrill, by the end of the filming of *Le Mans*, Steve had been given a bill by the IRS for $2 million. The $850,000 he would be paid for *Junior Bonner* was a start toward reviving his career and bank account.

The highest paid movie star in the world could still show his director and the cast who was the boss.

Unanswered phone calls became the first issue in their current relationship. It was the coming home scene with Ida. "I had a scene in mind of when I go to Mom's house and I have that scene with her which could be outside carrying tomatoes, in the kitchen she'd be kinda marvelous." Steve had given these thoughts in the Palm Springs meeting with Joe and Sam. In the revisions, I had written that scene, complete with the tomatoes, while adding Ace's dog, Dougal (fitted with false teeth to emphasize his growl).

Steve called Sam, he called me, and he called Ida. Sam and I were having a drink and dinner at the Palace. Ida was probably somewhere dining with Bob Preston.

The next morning, I showed up at the house chosen to be the Elvira Bonner home to discover a meeting to which I was not invited. Apparently, Steve was very upset no one answered his calls or even called him back. He needed a face-to-face with his director. Outside, the crew waited. I got eggs and a biscuit from the catering truck. Ida sat quietly in her chair reading a book.

The meeting took much of the morning. Not included, I never knew what all went on, especially to take up the entire morning. It turned out it had nothing to do with Steve's Junior finding his mother picking tomatoes and walking with her into the house, wanting to learn the whereabouts of his dad. That scene had already been filmed. Years later in a flashback to the *Grapes of Wrath* bulldozer scene, it was the poignant moment when Tom Joad first returned to meet his mother, the simple "Hello, Ma."

But now, in Steve's mind, it had everything to do with the dialogue that occurs with Ida in the kitchen, all over a slice of apple pie and a glass of milk.

We had shot the tomatoes scene the previous afternoon. It was as Steve had visualized in his notes: His mother is picking tomatoes, her son arrives, Dougal growls at him, he helps his mother carry the tomatoes into the house. Junior learns that Ace, none-too-sober, drove off the Cherry Creek Road, wrecked his pickup, is in the hospital and brother Curly is out promoting his new Reata Rancheros retirement community. Mom serves Junior apple pie and a glass of milk. So far, so good, but not for long. Steve kept changing his lines. Ida knew hers as written.

Message to me: Steve McQueen was letting his director and Ida Lupino know that he was the man who had made unanswered telephone calls, and if you don't respond, this is what you get.

Not one take was printed that afternoon. Every scene was a "hold." It was a wasted day. Uncomfortable for Ida, who was not going to change a written line, not even for Steve McQueen. And a message, in front of all, from Steve to Sam.

Yet the final word from Ida Lupino to Steve McQueen: "You damn well better know your lines tomorrow or you're going to eat one helluva lot of apple pie!"

Perhaps Ida Lupino was the real boss on this picture.

The next day the scene was printed in one take, including close-ups. It was done with the words written in the script. And only one glass of milk and one slice of apple pie.

I am certain this moment with Steve had to be vintage Ida, a pioneer for women directors with a reputation as a thorough professional.

Steve McQueen and knowing his lines as written was simply another day at the office.

It was during this time that Chalo Gonzalez arrived and was sent to stay in my room until proper lodgings could be found for him. Chalo was the uncle of Sam's second wife, Begonia Palacios. He had accomplished a brilliant scouting job of *The Wild Bunch* when Sam had refused location scouting help from Warner Brothers and sent Chalo on the mission. Chalo became indispensable to Sam. *Junior Bonner* was no exception. After two nights with me, a room was found for him and also a location job, to be paid for out of Sam's pocket. If you did not love Chalo, you found no love for humanity.

Dorothy and our daughter, Katherine, arrived in Prescott before the weekend. Their first stop was to celebrate our paycheck by visiting the Firestone dealer to buy four new tires for our Plymouth station wagon. Arriving at the Prescottonian in the early evening, who should the three of us meet but Steve? It was a moment we all fondly remember. I would later write in *Arizona Highways* magazine: "The four-year-old girl stood with her parents in a Prescott motel parking lot while they introduced her to the movie star."

Steve was friendly, gracious, and generous with his time. Just the four of us. As he was introduced to Katherine he placed his hand on her head. She was too shy to look up. "Katherine would always say she had met the highest-paid movie star in the world, Steve McQueen, but had never seen him," I wrote. It was a brief but telling moment about the side only those who share such a moment with Steve will ever know and forever remember.

That night we were awakened by the loudest screeching noise. It sounded like a child was being beaten. It went on for so long the Prescottonian emptied, with Bob, Ida, and others staring up toward our second floor. There, Casey Tibbs was unsuccessfully attempting to perch a rooster on the railing along the motel's second-floor walkway and a very stubborn rooster was loudly in refusal mode. Casey finally surrendered. He and the rooster disappeared into his room. We all returned to bed.

Not for long. The phone rang around 6:30 a.m. Sam was sending a driver over for me. I left Dorothy and Katherine behind.

Sam was in full mode to pit me against Joe Wizan. Sam ate breakfast from the pot of chili left on a low burner on the stove, where it remained, as he added to it, warming all summer. After a few minor production discussions—is this why the hell he wants me here at this hour of the morning? I wondered—the director swiftly got to the point. He produced the complete budget for the film. Did I know Joe and his partners charged ABC $100,000 for the script and received it, when, in reality, the script payment to me was but half that amount—and just what the hell was I going to do about it? I think he was surprised I did not appear angry or overly concerned. Hell, inwardly I was grateful to even be here, that my story and words were being filmed. Sam was a veteran of years of television and five major films with rewriting skills and paid-for screen credit on four of them.

Sam may have played the spider to the fly to me to create a fight with Joe Wizan, but he failed miserably. We went on to several other minor script issues, all positive, and his driver, Stacey Newton, returned me to the Prescottonian.

Over the years I learned Sam's true intention: to get me so angry at Joe, I would quit the picture then and there. Why? Because he wanted his great friend, New Mexico novelist (*The Rounders, The High Lo Country*) Max Evans there to spend the summer with him. Max, who has since become a very close friend to the Rosebrooks, wrote in his 2014 Peckinpah biography, *Goin' Crazy with Sam Peckinpah and All Our Friends*: "Sam called me and asked me to work on the script in Arizona. He offered me $1,000 a day and all the whiskey I could drink." Max also wrote: "*Junior Bonner* is the best rodeo film that's ever been made." He added. "It was the best script Sam ever got his hands on."

Into a memorable evening came the arrival of William Holden. The star of *The Wild Bunch* drove up from Palm Springs to visit Sam. Sam arranged for an outdoor catered dinner. We sat at a long table, side-by-side facing one another. Two events will always stand out to me: one is the motion picture history we absorbed as Ida, Bob, and Holden talked of their early studio days and, two, Holden's suddenly discovering Dorothy.

As the evening continued, Bill Holden moved himself all the way down the table to be beside Dorothy. I was across the table. I was ignored. About all I got in was how much I liked him in *Picnic* (1955). His reply before returning to Dorothy, "I was too old for that part."

Dorothy remembers as if it happened yesterday. "My wonderful visit with Bill Holden was a complete surprise as he was sitting at the other end of the table...the next thing I knew he was sitting next to me and introduced himself. Since this was my first time being involved with the filming of a movie...and a big star I had seen many times...I was surprised and he was just so natural and easy to talk with. We talked mostly about his place in Africa and how important it was to him. It was amazing and special to chat with him as he was like an old friend. Looking back, it was a very special moment in the years we spent in Hollywoodland. Wish I could have had more visits with him. He most likely moved down the table to me...I was thirty-three and not bad looking..."

While other conversations had continued, his was exclusively with her. And when our evening gathering with Bill Holden ended, he remained next to her. Within his handsome fifty-three-year-old looks, to me, there lived lonesome. Dorothy was real. Bill Holden, the man, not the actor, needed real. Holden was also going through a painful divorce from actress Brenda Marshall, a marriage of thirty years and four children.

While I worked, Dorothy shared a wonderful Saturday with Katherine, purchasing a colorful Southwestern-style dress. I joined them in time to walk together on the grassy lawns of the courthouse plaza. That evening, after dinner, when Katherine went to bed, we went downstairs to visit with Ida and Bob, who also came to Ida's room to visit. One of Dorothy's favorite memories of her Hollywood naiveté was mentioning Casey must be out on a date. They howled with laughter. In truth Casey's date, an extra from Van Nuys, was upstairs undoubtedly pleasuring Possibly America's Most Beloved Cowboy.

We looked outside to see Katherine in her blanket. She had wandered down the stairs looking for us. Ida promptly swooped

Katherine up in her arms. We spent the evening talking, sharing a glass of wine, with Ida cradling Katherine to her.

Time out of time, making a Hollywood movie.

Sunday arrived and Don "Red" Barry had arranged an auction to benefit the Boys' Club of Prescott. Wardrobe items from the actors were to be auctioned off for a deserving charity. The star attraction was to be Casey's rooster! Casey had his rooster living in the basement of the Palace, but now it was to be auctioned off as a "movie rooster" who worked for $40 a day. We left Katherine with Frank Kowalski's daughter as her babysitter.

We all awaited the movie rooster's appearance. This was to be the grand finale. Casey, who was drinking Champale, sat back to watch Don sell the prized rooster to the crowd. Don explained to all that the "movie rooster" was trained to perch on his microphone. Thus began Don's challenge to accomplish such a feat. Laughter filled the room as Don gave the effort his all, but the rooster was totally uncooperative. The more uncooperative, the more laughter continued to grow and the more Casey became irritated. With his reputation at stake, Casey gave up his Champale long enough to head up to the stage and the microphone. Relieving Don of the rooster, announcing his movie rooster earned $40 a day on the picture, Possibly America's Most Beloved Cowboy perched his rooster on the microphone and there, until a bid of $400 was given and accepted, it remained.

The rooster never "worked" a day.

There followed our day at the horse races at the fairgrounds. While the rodeo was an annual Prescott Fourth of July feature lasting a good portion of a week, the horse races—thoroughbreds, and quarter horses—continued daily for much of the summer. Frank Kowalski, his wife, Emma, an important part of John Wayne's Batjack Productions back in Los Angeles; Dorothy and me; and Elsa Cardenas, whom Sam had cast in *The Wild Bunch*, all filled a box seat at the edge of the track. (Frank's daughter was caring for Katherine.) Sam bet on every horse in every race. He had to win something, of course, and in his celebratory mood, announced he was having a barbecue that night at his rented house.

As we were leaving the track, Sam found another thoughtful way—the way his mind worked—to rid himself of me. He stopped at the gate to the track and made a serious announcement with the well-shaped, thirty-five-year-old Elsa Cardenas beside him. (Elsa was an actress and known to have been intimate with Elvis Presley and director Budd Boetticher during the 1960s before Sam.) "Jeb," announced Sam, "is going to Hawaii tomorrow with Elsa. Dorothy is staying with me."

Thanks, but no thanks, Sam.

But if I had accepted? If I had said it sounded like a good plan? Two strikes on Sam.

Sam's barbecue, with him as the chef, went on later than anyone, except Sam, had planned. We had to film drive shots on Highway 89A north of Prescott early the next day. Sam and Casey, continuing from his Champale time at the auction, were drinking the hard stuff more than the others.

I was nearby when words were exchanged between Casey and Sam. It had something to do with the next day's morning shoot. Casey was to get in his best clothes and boots for the drive shots. Somehow, it sounded like a storm was brewing between them.

Casey later told Peckinpah biographer Garner Simmons, "I think I put it to him one night when we weren't too far from throwin' fists. I liked the picture and I liked the job, but I wasn't gonna get completely stomped down and I told Sam, 'One thing about it, we've all got a helluva break.' And Sam says, 'What's that?' And I said, "Cause you weigh about 140 pounds and if you weighed 200, you'd charge everybody in the world $5 an hour to live!'"

No more was said between them. Casey told me he had once asked a director how his hemorrhoids were behaving. The director replied he did not have hemorrhoids, to which Casey responded, "Good. I always knew you were a perfect asshole."

Casey had had his say. As far as I could tell, nothing further was said between them. Casey had been drinking much of Sunday afternoon and into that evening. Likewise, Sam Peckinpah.

When Dorothy and I were in the car ready to leave, she suddenly said she had not said goodnight to Sam and needed to do so. I directly replied that this was most definitely not a good idea.

Unconvinced of my warning, off she went into the night to bid fare-well to Sam Peckinpah. When she returned, she exclaimed, with shock and yet without anger, "He stuck his tongue in my mouth!"

"Well, I warned you," I replied. Strike two-and-a-half.

Dorothy at thirty-three, was a beautiful blonde. Her personality was genuine and without any hint of Hollywood bullshit. This trait had already endeared her to Bob and Ida. And, of course, to William Holden. Dorothy Rosebrook, the Chosen One!

When Dorothy and Katherine left the next morning I was left alone with the thought of where my future days were going with Sam. The spider to the fly had tested my marriage by taking an out-side chance I might wish to enter his world of varietal sex by whisk-ing off to Hawaii with Elsa Cardenas (I'm sure these travel plans were the first she'd heard about them), and then giving Dorothy a French kiss, perhaps giving a thought that I might challenge him, as Casey had done that evening.

I was not from his world of Begonia, Elsa, Joie, Mary Murphy, and, the one who cared genuinely for him the most, Katy Haber. If he could have seduced Dorothy into his world of any possible kind of sex, it would have joined the universe of Peckinpah women, including the Tennessee Williams dread he may have felt for his mother.

Dorothy would not spend time with Sam again until his fiftieth birthday party, five years later. Her impressions of Sam in Prescott remain very clear: "Sam was full of himself...lots of needy atten-tion. He was most likely very creative and bright...wanted to shock me, as I was truly a very square proper person. He enjoyed engaging in conversation with me...pushy and wanted to see what I would do when he proposed outrageous things...such as sending you to Hawaii with one of his many girlfriends and me staying with him.

"He respected you and me...we were the opposite of his lifestyle."

Dorothy and Katherine were gone and by that hot Monday morning, the crew was gathered within the trees for the drive shots along Highway 89A. As requested, Casey arrived dressed in his best Western suit and the Paul Bond boots he called his "dancing slippers," as befitting Possibly America's Most Beloved Cowboy. Sam might have been waiting for some reaction from me about Dorothy and the day and night before. There was none. I stood close by Lucien and the camera crew, and what I saw was Sam's humiliation of Casey Tibbs.

Sam had not forgotten Casey's words from the night before. Casey was assigned to ride in a station wagon in the passenger seat. The camera never got within one hundred yards of the station wagon—not close enough to even recognize who was in it.

The winner, at 140 pounds!

It was time to get back to the action of the rodeo grounds. Ben Johnson, as rodeo stock contractor, Buck Roan, arrives. We are reintroduced to Sunshine, the menace and danger of the black Brahma bull. Steve to test his strength finds the bull alone in a corral. He climbs the fence into the corral. Give credit to Steve. There was no way to film the challenge between man and bull with a stunt double. Steve eased himself closer to Sunshine. The bull backed up and pawed the ground. They faced one another. Steve, finding within himself the character needed for Junior, held his ground. When Sunshine made his move to charge, Steve, staying within character, headed for the fence, much to the enjoyment of those gathered to watch the moment, including Ben and Casey.

Building on this, important, emotional scenes for Steve were to come.

But first was Buck Hart, my longtime kazoo-playing West Virginia-born cowboy/English teacher at the Orme School. Hired by Lynn Stallmaster to assist in casting locals, Buck was chosen for a brief scene feeding the bucking stock in the fairgrounds, tossing hay from the back of a pickup truck. As the scene was written, Buck was to be singing the Stan Jones song "Cowpoke," made popular by Rex Allen in 1951, the lyrics engrained in my mind from the days listening to the radio when milking cows at Orme School, "I'll pick up a ten spot, In Prescott I know, I'll ride in the broncs, In the big rodeo...."

Prior to the scene, I am called to meet with Sam.

Buck stands frozen in place before Sam.

Sam lets out his fury on me. "He doesn't know the goddamn song!"

What am I to say? A verse from the Rex Allen song was in the original script. Was Buck so honored he forgot to learn the words?

"He doesn't know the goddamn fucking words."

I am ordered to take Buck over by the corrals and teach him the words.

No, there is not enough time. Fuck the words. Get him in the corral.

So Buck goes into the corral, on the back of the truck. "Come get it, boys!" he choruses as he tosses out the hay.

What neither Buck nor I knew was that the picture never intended to use the words from the Rex Allen song, as it was too expensive.

Yet for Buck Hart, it was a glorious day that had begun in makeup early in the morning with Robert Preston and would continue later in the day sitting in the Buck Roan Cadillac with Ben Johnson.

These were moments that genuinely touched Buck Hart for the rest of his life.

What Sam had found in his element in Prescott was the use of locals, not totally as extras, but in speaking parts.

Take the case of a recently retired cowboy named Alex. Alex was tall, lean, and with a distinctive face and voice. I am uncertain just where Sam found him to use in a moment with Bob Preston as Ace. Ace is about to ride from the rodeo grounds to join the parade on Junior's horse alongside the barrel-racing twins ("Are you JR's dad?").

Alex, playing the character of Roy, took several takes because his instinct was to look at the camera and not up at Ace, horseback. Here was another Sam—instinctively, the Sam who grew up on a family ranch east of Fresno, California, in the Sierra Nevada in the company of real cowboys. Sam was gentle with "Roy," easing him into the scene with Ace asking, "How many parades we been in, Roy?" (Roy's reply in the script is "Not enough, Ace.") As I recall, as Ace rode away, bound for the parade, Roy replied, "Maybe not enough, maybe too many."

Roy and that moment were pure Peckinpah genius. Other than *Straw Dogs*, made in England, he had never made a film set in America's contemporary world. With that came the opportunity to use the real people of the real West of the 1970s.

Meanwhile, Steve was getting into the depth that was Junior. Marty Baum's casting instincts had been correct—other than his misadventure with Ida, the trio of Steve, Ida, and Bob were bringing forth honest screen chemistry. When the company moved into a dinner sequence in the home Elvira Bonner had once shared with Ace and was now also an antiques shop, Steve delivered a brilliant low-key performance as he ate his pork chops and mashed potatoes.

Save for Ace, who was in the hospital, the family was gathered. Steve and Joe Don Baker had discovered their chemistry at the Reata Rancheros sequence when brother and brother, potential real estate millionaire and older brother journeyman rodeo cowboy first met. At the table, Joe Don, as brother Curly, drank bourbon whiskey and touted his success. Mary Murphy had one of Steve's favorite lines when she admonished her mother-in-law, who, feeding her infant in a high-chair, lit up a cigarillo, "Mom, do you have to smoke when you're feeding our baby?" One of their two sons at the table, young Matthew Peckinpah, had one of his father's lines when Junior offers the boys rodeo tickets, "You can ride anything that's got hair on it."

It was a scene such as this one, and more to come, that provided Steve with among the best acting performances in his career. And this scene, and one shortly thereafter in which Junior punches out brother Curly, establishes the dysfunctional but loving unit of the Bonner family.

The past history of *The Cincinnati Kid*, however, would always linger. Sam professionally directed Steve. Steve, as reported in Marshall Terrill's biography, referred to Sam as "Mr. Peckinpah." So far, they got along. But how long will this last?

While Steve was enjoying his new private life with Barbara in Prescott, and even having his children, Terry and Chad, visit briefly, he worked hard each day, bringing genuine depth to his performance as Junior. Sam was becoming more erratic and angry as he put first assistant directors and other crew members into his barrel or worse—on the bus.

The first was an American Film Institute intern, a young black man assigned by AFI executive and a friend of Sam's, Jim Silke, to the film. The intern was told by Sam (as he told me) to always be beside him. I cannot remember the details. But as with the brief tour of duty by second unit director Carroll Ballard, the intern's fate, for whatever reason, was sealed. Ray Green, an assistant to Joe Wizan, was the only other black man on the film. I found Ray a terrific person and one I knew had a great career ahead of him. The intern was not fitting in. Granted, Prescott was not the most comfortable place in 1971 for a young African-American assigned to shadow the potentially ever-volatility that was Sam Peckinpah.

There came one day on the steps of the Yavapai County Court-house when Sam commanded dutiful observance from his intern in front of the entire cast and crew.

That was the last we saw of our intern.

Sam was further displeased, for whatever reason, with assistant director Michael Messinger. He was slated for the bus, yet was saved from his fate by Frank Kowalski, who promised Sam to keep Mike out of his sight. Sam reluctantly agreed. Mike's time in Prescott was saved. For now. (Mike would return to Hollywood and a successful career as an assistant director, which had started in 1956, until a debilitating injury forced him to retire from the industry in 1981. He died May 13, 2017.)

Marty Baum's strategy to strengthen the casting was again proven with the arrival of Sandra Deel, a forty-three-year-old Manhattan-based actress and singer with a television and Broadway pedigree going back to the 1950s. She was playing Nurse Arlis, who had found Ace as her patient in the hospital and was well on her way to capturing his heart. In one of his lighter, genuine Bob Preston moments, Ace pats Arlis on the behind with the line, "My hand on your heart." I remember being one of the first to greet Sandra upon her arrival in Prescott. Tall and angular, Sandra, perfectly cast, had a very special look to her, and a wonderful sense of humor to play between Ace and Elvira.

Sam had his hires with Lucien, Ben, Mary Murphy principally, with Joe Don Baker and Bill McKinney Lyn Stallmaster agreed-upon casting with Sam, Marty, and Joe Wizan.

And Steve had Barbara.

And Sam had wonderful, devoted Katy Haber.

***

From the production standpoint, the film was moving on sched-ule, save for the loss of some time due to rain. Bill Pierce was ever there to deliver Steve's paycheck (who recalled to me forty years lat-er every one of them was a six-figure check) and continue to keep open the old dirt track for Steve to share energy with his motor-cycle. Barbara left the Prescottonian to move in with Steve. "Every morning in Steve's trailer, we shared breakfast while he went over his lines," Barbara related to co-author Marshall Terrill in *The King, McQueen and the Love Machine.* "And I went over mine if I had any scenes for that day. Sam was always waiting for us to arrive. "Things started to happen whenever Steve walked onto the set; he was the real boss and everyone knew it."

For me, the reality of Steve McQueen, at this time when he was piecing his life together for a new future, was the scene with Ben Johnson when Junior reveals his need to ride Sunshine in front of his hometown people. The stock contractor can make no promises to Junior as to gaining the draw to ride the bull. For Junior it is only a matter of pride and not the prize money as he tells Ben, "Money's nobody's favor."

The beauty of that scene is that no two actors could ever have more respect for one another than Steve and Ben, as Junior and Buck.

Steve equally endeared himself to the rodeo cowboys when, on a bucking horse in the chute, he either on purpose or accidentally spurred the bronc, causing the horse to suddenly rear. The look on Steve's face says it all. It certainly wasn't in the script.

He also took over when Sam found Barbara's acting ability in need when she was not looking concerned enough as Steve is thrown from a bronc. He continued to have her redo the moment to a point considered "spiteful." She revealed that Steve took over directing at that moment.

I was never aware of what happened. She said it was an arrangement previously made by Steve and Sam, who was furious he wasn't able to hire another actress. It must have embarrassed Sam in front of the crew.

Then Sam was left out of a party given by Bob and Ida for Hair and Wardrobe staffers one Saturday night, in gratitude for these behind-the-scenes people.

My friend R. Kirk (Sandy) Dunbar had driven up from Phoenix. R. Kirk had been responsible for so much of all this when we drove up the previous year to attend the rodeo.

We were at the Palace having a drink. Sam was drinking with Katy and other crew members. He had an "office" upstairs in one of the rooms above the Palace. He was paying particular attention to a young, heavyset Native American woman, who was dressed in less-than-attractive clothes. He suddenly made the decision we all had to attend Bob and Ida's party up the road at the Pine Cone Inn.

I had no idea that Bob and Ida were giving such a party. So we all went. It was totally embarrassing to me. Sam was in jeans and his working clothes from the day. Coming into the restaurant it was obvious, with the Native woman Sam made a show of, that he had arrived with his power play at not being included. Wardrobe, Makeup, and Hair staff members, as well as Bob, Ida, and Sandra Deel, were dressed in their finest for the dinner. We had dinner with them.

What was intended as a fine evening sponsored by Bob and Ida, turned awkward, very awkward. But Sam Peckinpah was their director.

This moment left me knowing allegiance to a paycheck was with Sam. Allegiance on a personal and professional level was unquestionably with Bob Preston and Ida Lupino.

Bob and Ida took it all in stride, keeping their feelings to themselves. Bob had been making films since 1938, Ida since 1934. Additionally, Bob was a Broadway star, winning two Tony Awards for *The Music Man* and *I Do, I Do,* while Ida was well-known as a director. Looking back on that evening, I realize now that these two actors, chosen for Marty Baum's strategy of building a strong acting cast around Steve, did not need Sam Peckinpah. He needed them. Ida had already once put Sam in his place. In *Ida Lupino,* Robert Donati's biography of the actress, he writes: "On the first day of shooting, before the cameras rolled, Peckinpah made a sarcastic remark about her lipstick, which embarrassed Ida before two hundred cast and crew members. She angrily confronted the director, threatening to quit. Only roses, champagne, and an apology brought her back." (I do not recall being present, but have no doubt Sam's intent was to show who was in charge, perhaps inwardly feeling inferior to her years of experience, especially as a director.)

When Sam's power play was complete, we left the Pine Cone Inn, returning to the Palace for more party. R. Kirk seemed intrigued. Exhausted from the day's work, I begged off, returning to my motel.

It was not long before R. Kirk returned to the Prescottonian. When the party moved upstairs to Sam's "office," R. Kirk, who nobody knew other than as a newcomer friend of mine, was verbally told he was excluded.

The anger within Sam, fueled by alcohol, which Katy Haber had known since episodes on *Straw Dogs* in England, took over. The weekend before with too much to drink, he had nearly come to blows with Casey and he had French-kissed Dorothy. Tonight he had brought a female companion to invade the well-dressed party hosted by two of his actors, in a show of power. Tonight he would be upstairs in the Palace with Katy—and others who often stayed up with him late into the night. No matter what the occasion, or how late they stayed up, Sam was always on time for work the next day.

***

Sunday. A work day, making up for a day when rain delayed outdoor filming.

The only cast member involved was Steve.

Katy showed up with a very bruised chin.

I remembered that day walking with Sam to lunch when he'd said, "I hit Joie."

Steve asked, "What happened to you?"

Katy replied, "I fell down."

"You usually do," Steve responded, "when you get hit."

It was not an eventful day. I rode with Steve in his Winnebago with Joe's assistant, Betty Gumm, and production secretary Dorothy Whitney. My impression was that Steve seemed to have Dorothy Whitney on his radar. I also recall he was cordial to Sam, but coolly cordial. Sam, behind his dark glasses, must have been suffering a brutal hangover. Katy, ever loyal, stood by Sam. Steve said nothing. One could ask how he could be offended when only a year ago in France, during the making of *Le Mans*, he had held a revolver to his wife's head, both high on cocaine, when she revealed a one-time affair to actor Maximilian Schell. A likely answer in my mind was that his wife Neile was fading from his life, Barbara was today, and this Steve McQueen, now forty years old, was—he honestly believed—a new Steve McQueen.

Lucien Ballard and the crew had also seen Katy.

Later that day, the creative power living within Sam took over. He asked me to have a drink with him at the Palace. The next day we were scheduled to film the all-important father/son scene at the Santa Fe railroad depot. Sam recounted how his father, when he disappointed him as a boy, would cuff his hat off. This is what Sam wanted Ace to do. When Ace learns from his son, Junior, that he has no money to send him to Australia, he'd cuff his hat off. As Sam recalled this moment with his own father, he was visibly emotionally affected. He was a rancher's son on a land he loved.

I never mentioned Katy to Sam. Yet in the forefront of Sam's mind had to be the knowledge that Steve and Lucien and his crew had seen the bruised chin and soon his actors would see Katy. What was done, was done. Sadly, these were different times.

Monday morning came and with it, rehearsing the depot scene between Steve and Bob.

Steve was shirtless with a cup of tea. The dialogue was all there. In a reprise of Ida's apple pie day with him, Steve made the rehearsal difficult by wanting to change his lines. Bob was patient as Sam continued to press to do the scene as written.

I quickly realized that Steve was doing what he was doing because he knew Sam had hit Katy. The rehearsal dragged on. Finally, Steve knew he had taken up enough of Bob's time and accepted the scene as written.

In one final act of showing how he felt, Steve walked away from us, taking his cup of tea and letting the tea fly over his shoulder toward Sam. It wasn't the scene. It was about Katy.

The depot scene, with father and son sitting on a station bench, Junior's saddled horse behind them, fresh from their wild ride through the backyards of Prescott (a pickup from the parade scene) became one of the highlights of the film and a centerpiece of Steve's performance. The painful memory Steve had of the non-existence of a real father, surfaced in Junior's character in this scene with Ace. Bob's portrayal of Ace brought the emotion of father and son to absolute reality. Curly was placing Ace on a weekly allowance. Junior revealed he had no money to help his dad achieve his Australian dream.

A train engine is coming. Ace, in the frustration of the moment, cuffs his hat off. It lands across the tracks. Ace walks slowly across the tracks, heavy with disappointment. The train engine comes between them. Steve leans away. For perhaps the first time in his career, Steve McQueen is seen close to or with tears in his eyes.

At the end of the scene, as the train engine has passed, Ace returns with the hat. And Junior announces, "If you're not too old" he has entered them in the wild cow-milking competition.

The bruise on Katy's chin was more than a clear advertisement that Sam had crossed the line. Yet no matter how any of the crew felt, they all knew we had to stay on schedule.

So on to the wild cow-milking sequence at the rodeo grounds. In today's professional rodeo world, when this event is held, a cow is let loose, the roper ropes the cow, his partner races with a small bottle to drain some milk from cow, and then runs as fast as he can back to a finish line.

In previous times, those I knew, practically a herd of cows was let loose at once. Ropers moved in to rope a cow. Their partners, called "muggers," raced in to hold the cow long enough for the roper to dismount, grab the bottle, assuming the mugger got some milk, and run like hell for a finish line.

Knowing I had grown up on a nearby ranch, Sam decided to "try me." He had six ropers and six muggers. I was to be the seventh mugger just, perhaps, to create some confusion among us all.

Fitted with a pair of boots, I was ready. The day was very hot. The "bad" Dougal dog was about to join us. Ross Dollarhide, who had drawn praise from Sam for his stunt double work for Bob Preston, with his Ace wig on, was ready to do his roping as the camera followed him into the oncoming chaos.

But Ross missed his loop.

Put all the cows back in the corral. Muggers, back to your places. The cows are again let loose. Muggers run to join in.

But Ross again misses his loop.

Sam is beside himself. Ross is in disgrace. Mickey Gilbert, our stunt coordinator, the man who hired Ross, is ordered to wear Ace's wardrobe, wig, and hat.

And we do it again.

This time Mickey ropes the cow. All hell breaks loose. Dougal races within the mass of cattle and dust, jumping to bite cowboys and racing after the cows, barking and growling. Within all this, I find a cow. I grab it in bulldog position around the horns. The cow takes me on a ride, but I hold on, yelling for someone to milk my cow.

When it is all over, the cowboys are laughing their asses off at me. My cow had already been milked.

My time with that cow was forever immortalized when Sam left that moment in the film.

Most important to me: Sam had "tried me." And he knew I could handle myself.

I had never attempted to grab a fully grown cow by the horns and throw it down. This part was brand new. But I had gone to the Quarter Circle V Bar Ranch School when I was nine. From that age on I was on round-ups in the fall and spring. There were times on November fall round-ups when it was so cold, other kids were crying in the saddle. There were no zippers on Levis in those days, only metal buttons. In the cold weather, it was no easy task to unbutton your fly if you had to pee, and God only knows how difficult it was for the girls, if any of them tried.

The Orme Family took us out of school to do the East Pasture, the Taylor Place Pasture, Osborne Wash Pasture, the CCC Tank Pasture, and the West Pasture. We were up at five, took flashlights into the corral to find and catch our horses, saddled up, had breakfast, then rode out with sunrise. Most often we drove the cattle back to the ranch by noon or soon thereafter, although there were times when, at Taylor Place or West, one of the senior Ormes—Aunt Minna or Uncle Chick—drove a truck with a lunch of frijoles and cornbread to the branding corrals. Branding took much of the afternoon and we all took part: castration, ear-marking, de-horning, vaccinating, and branding, with black bug medicine painted over the branding, de-horning, ear marking, and brand. We fell asleep at night to the sounds of mother cows mourning the loss of calves weaned from them that day. As I recall, there were not so many male calves chosen to be bulls with the year branded below the Quarter Circle V Bar.

I'm sure Sam had many similar experiences growing up. He put me into the scene to see for himself if there could be a cowhand side to me. The other cow-milkers also accepted me as real. Thus Sam preserved an homage to my time with that cow for the final cut of the film: the guy with the dark black hair and a blue shirt.

In a sense, I had pulled even with Sam in being tested. I had become respected for real, and not just for writing, by Casey, Ben, Ross, Mickey Gilbert, and the other stunt cowboys.

But as I would learn, my time of being tested by Sam was not over.

As John Ford before him had depended on cinematographers Winston Hoch and Archie Stout, so Sam's career had been enhanced previously by Lucien Ballard. I often watched the two of them together. I studied them as a team. Both were listeners to the other. Barbara Leigh may have stated that when Steve arrived on the set, the crew knew who was boss. This did not include Lucien.

Steve knew Lucien from *Nevada Smith* for which Lucien was there, framing every shot in the film with iconic director Henry Hathaway. If anything, Steve, like the crew, perhaps deferred more to Lucien than to Sam. Yet Lucien had found Sam's choice of material a perfect match for his cameras and each made the other better for it.

I found this tall, imperiously reserved man to be the epitome of the word "class." I had a chance to share lunch twice with Lucien and his wife, Inez, a short, attractive, quiet woman, who was more than modest, considering her accomplishments. While Lucien filmed movie adventures, Inez lived one of the most dangerous adventures ever in the world.

"Read *The Rivers Ran East*," suggested Lucien at one of these luncheons at their rental home in Prescott. "Inez is the first woman to travel up to the headwaters of the Amazon." Absolutely true. In a recent edition of Leonard Clark's dangerous journey of discovery, *Travelers' Tales*, Executive Editor Larry Hasegger writes: "…fearless Inez Pokorny," who with Leonard Clark, "forge their way through a violent world where disaster lurks around every bend in the river: man eating jaguars, giant anacondas, headhunting Indians, and poisonous creatures of every sort."

On the set, Lucien always carried a slim swagger stick. In fact, he had a supply of them, should one be broken. One was broken as an attractive young extra strolled past. Receiving a gentle swat of admiration on her behind, the young woman grabbed hold of Lucien's swagger stick and broke it. As I recall, she was not seen again in another scene.

"Go in there," Sam said, as our car stopped in front of the Palace, "and tell McKinney his lines are cut." Did Sam not want to face the outward toughness that the Tennessee actor was known for since his recent badass (no pun intended) role in *Deliverance*? Or was he teaching a writer the face-to-face dealings he will face in the future with actors and words? I had gotten to know Bill and we got along fine. As the character of Red Terwiliger, he was Junior's main rodeo rival, and most of his lines applied to that relationship. Into the Palace I went, the bearer of bad news for any actor. Bill simply nodded. I waited for blowback, but there was none. Of course, it helped that I told him it was Sam's decision.

Bill's roomie at the Prescottonian was the soft-spoken Texas native Joe Don Baker, who played Curly. Like McKinney, Joe Don was physically not one to be trifled with. Now eighty years old, Joe Don looked back on his experience in the film. "Sam was a prick," he said, "and an asshole. But he's dead now and there's no point talking over the dead." He elaborated: "I didn't care for Peckinpah at all. He was one of those little guys who tries to bully big guys and he almost got his ass whipped for trying to bully me." Joe Don was referring to the Palace scene in which Steve knocks him down after this brotherly reminder: "I'm working on my first million and you are still working on eight seconds." Sam made Joe Don do the scene many times over. In my memory, the first take was good enough to print. "Every time I was going to throttle Peckinpah, Steve McQueen would come over and calm me down like a brother would."

Joe Don enjoyed his time in Prescott that summer, although in a scene with Steve as Curly is selling retirement homes at Reata Rancheros, he had to do the scene over when he first pronounced Prescott as "Pres-cot" and had to be reminded by a local (or perhaps it was me) that the correct local pronunciation is "Pres-kit, like biscuit."

Joe Don's experience is reminiscent of the bullying Robert Ryan took on location with *The Wild Bunch* in Mexico. In J.R. Jones's biography, *The Lives of Robert Ryan*, William Holden biographer

Bob Thomas wrote: "After the company moved to Torreon, Ryan asked Peckinpah for a few days off so he could do some campaigning." (Ryan, an ex-Marine and confirmed liberal, wanted to assist in Democratic campaigning in California.) Sam turned him down. The actor thus reported on the set in makeup and costume for ten days. He was never used. Finally, he grabbed Peckinpah by the shirt-front and growled, "I'll do anything you ask me to do in front of the camera, because I'm a professional. But you open your mouth to me off the set and I'll knock your teeth in.'"

About me being sent on the errand to cut McKinney's lines, Baker recalls, "There was a blond actress Sam thought Bill was screwing. I don't know whether Sam was screwing her or not, but because of what he thought Bill was doing, he cut all his lines."

So it stands to reason, there was more than just acting in my assignment to cut McKinney's lines, which is probably why he accepted the news without a fight.

Meanwhile, Sam's second unit director and longtime friend, Frank Kowalski, had kept his word in keeping first assistant director Michael Messinger out of Sam's sight and mind, until one evening when Sam invited us all for a drink at a local bar to play Liar's Poker. The game had become the way to pass time, using per diem dollars or otherwise, in which the player picks a dollar bill from his bills and, without looking at the serial numbers, challenges his opponent to call him a liar when he foretells he has, say, "five threes," not knowing if he really has them.

When Michael entered the bar, Sam, spotting him, invited the young assistant director to join us in the game. Pleased that he was now recognized by his director, Michael was eager to accept. The problem being, Michael really did not fully understand the game: i.e., you were not to look at the numbers on your bill. Thus it was Michael who took a bill from his wallet, momentarily eyed it, long enough for Sam to accuse him of cheating.

"On the bus," he said. And so it was.

On the following Saturday night, Frank Kowalski borrowed Sam's Porsche so that the two of us could go out to dinner. It was a quiet evening, with only a drink or two at a small Italian restaurant in downtown Prescott.

On Sunday morning, Frank stopped by my room.

"Farewell, top hat and tails!" he announced.

What? Sam's closest friend, together with Chalo—Frank had been with Sam since *The Wild Bunch*. Frank had then, with Vic Morrow, written the Western *A Man Called Sledge* (1970) and was currently working with Sam on a proposed film, *Bring Me the Head of Alfredo Garcia* (1974), for which Frank had created the story. Like Chalo, where Sam Peckinpah went, so went the talented Frank Kowalski as second unit director, dialogue coach or director, location manager. He had spent part of the summer down the street at a different motel with his wife, Emma, and daughter. They had returned to L.A., leaving Frank with lots of work as second unit director but with his wages garnished by Vic Morrow, due to a dispute between them over *Sledge*.

What had happened? Sam had fired someone as close and valuable to him as Frank Kowalski?

I am, after all these years, unclear of the "why." Frank's version was that Sam accused him of overdrinking while out with me the night before and driving his car while intoxicated. (Not true, as I was with Frank.) But it may have been Sam's excuse, as Frank did not come as he was told to a production meeting that morning. Sam told biographer Garner Simmons that Frank told him he could not make it, due to overdrinking the night before. Had he gone somewhere else in Sam's Porsche after he dropped me off? Sam also indicated to Simmons that Frank had been doing a "half-bad" job—"thousands of feet of film." When Frank made it clear he was not coming to the production meeting, Sam made the decision to fire him.

On the bus. Or in this case—"top hat and tails, and farewell!"

Relationships come and go among a location film crew. And with some, they remain close beyond one film and one location. So it was with Dorothy and Jeb and Frank and Emma Kowalski.

Losing assistant directors was now contagious.

Then, two new true professionals arrived: Newt Arnold and Malcomb "Mack" Harding. Newt not only lasted, but would join Sam on future films. Mack was a stand-up Westerner with plenty of backbone—there was no way Sam will trifle with these two. Both were veterans.

Joe Wizan told Simmons: "Sam works from an emotional level rather than from an intellectual one. One of the things I like about working with him is that there is no theorizing. He can talk intellectually with you on almost any subject, but he doesn't direct that way."

Yet Joe left most of his day-to-day on-the-set chores to his best friend and associate producer, Mickey Borofsky. Joe and the company did well filling in the assistant director roles of those fired.

Within the schedule for filming, there was ahead one week in the Palace Bar, a major brawl involving us all, an event invented by Sam to replace much of the relationship scenes between Junior and Charmagne in the original script.

Joe Wizan knew Sam Peckinpah worked from his gut. Sam's gut told him Jeb Rosebrook was acting like a playwright in bringing a one-night-stand relationship together with Junior and Charmagne. After all, he had changed Barbara Leigh's character from a young woman driving up to the rodeo in Prescott in her VW Bug to a high fashion, sexy woman on the arm of a wealthy wheeler-dealer. For Barbara, Elvis had been left behind in real life, and now she belonged to Steve McQueen. She was certainly a beauty to be fought over, and so it would be.

It would all take place when the rodeo announcer tells the crowd it is time to take a break and go down to the Palace—the "half time" break I believed rodeo purists would be up in arms about, and rightfully so.

The word went out to the people of Prescott and beyond—extras needed in the Palace to duplicate the drinking and dancing that, in real life, had taken place over the Fourth. It was a great time for people in Prescott to sign up, including a number of local Native Americans, including one young man who worked nearby ranches, known to me only by his first name, Curtis. It was now time for Stunt Coordinator Mickey Gilbert, thirty-four, to take over in the principal role as choreographer of the fight, which would take place within the entire Palace Saloon.

To prepare the Prescott locals, men and women and those of us who would be the amateur stuntmen, Mickey took us to the Prescott YMCA. "I offered the locals five dollars a day for our practice fight and how to be a part of actually duplicating the real thing," Gilbert recalls, now eighty years old. Mickey Gilbert was the true professional, having risen from a 1956 bareback bronc riding champion on the rodeo circuit to becoming one of the most sought-after stunt professionals in Hollywood. He had first worked with Sam on *The Wild Bunch*, in which he doubled for, as he remembers, "forty-two Mexicans."

"Joe Wizan and [production manager] Jim Pratt heard about me paying all these people five dollars a day and called a meeting as to why I was spending their money this way, and without their permission." Mickey remembers telling them: "If they don't really know what to do and how to do it, you will have to do a lot of re-shooting. It could cost you $25,000 a day."

Permission granted!

Going back to their first meeting on *The Wild Bunch*, Sam had total confidence in Mickey Gilbert. "I remember on *The Wild Bunch* everyone was afraid of Sam. I wasn't. He didn't know me, but I had an idea for a gag [a stunt] and went right up to him and introduced myself." At first skeptical of Mickey's idea, to have a horse fall and drag with money from the robbery in the film's opening, Sam gave his okay. The stunt worked. From that time on, Sam Peckinpah was well aware of who Mickey Gilbert was and what he was all about.

"When Sam hired me, I went over to Prescott before the filming began to meet him. I was told he was at a motel [doubtless, the Prescottonian] and I went out there. Joe Wizan and Jim Pratt were in a limo waiting to see him. 'You'll have to wait, they told me. He's not ready to see us,' they told me.'" Mickey was not about to wait. He went to Sam's room and knocked on the door. "He opened the door and was buck naked. I think with a chick in there," Mickey remembers. "I just wanted to let you know I was here," Mickey told him. In his autobiography, *Me and My Saddle Pal*, Mickey writes that Sam then "breezily" waved out to Wizan and Pratt, saying, "I'll be right with you guys." Going back to their first meeting on *The Wild Bunch*, Mickey says, "I liked the way he worked." So it came about that Mickey would reunite with Sam in Prescott.

We had a meeting at the Palace on that Sunday afternoon, the day before filming the fight began. Before I got there, Mickey was working closely with Sam in making final plans. They were together in a booth at the Palace. There was only one distraction. Their meeting was interrupted by Sam "seeing Katy at the bar talking to a sailor." In a rage of jealousy, startling Mickey, "he went over and jerked her off her bar stool and brought her over to our meeting."

When I arrived for the meeting, Sam was saying he needed to add a bouncer to the fight. A big brawler, the biggest of them all. As Sam had created retired cowboy Alex into Roy, so now he knew in his gut there would be a place for another real life local.

Sam sent someone next door to Matt's Saloon, and thus returned "Big Jim," who happened to be the Sunday replacement for the regular bouncer at Matt's. Jim worked construction and was totally taken by surprise to be offered the role. He would enter the Palace, as Mickey worked it out with Sam, turn over the pool table and establish that he was the man to bring an end to our brawl. He would surely make his presence felt by all. And, as Mickey choreographed it, he'd put an emphatic end to the fight. Big Jim's presence would end it all.

As we sat there that Sunday afternoon, just as I had sat with Sam when he felt the emotional addition to the depot scene was the cuffing off of Junior's hat, he was again organizing, collaborating with his valuable stunt coordinator, acting as commander-in-chief of one of the biggest movie brawls ever. John Ford would have been proud.

Only three professional stuntmen would be involved. One of them was Jimmy Sheppard, who had suffered stuntman trauma when, in *The Wild Bunch*, he was one of the riders when the bridge they were crossing blew up and all riders and horses plunged into the river below. Mickey knew the trauma inflicted on Jimmy. He knew Jimmy needed work. He brought him to Prescott. He and Jimmy had become close since their time together in Mexico on *The Wild Bunch*. There were about six more of us who also would act as stuntmen reacting as such when the brawl broke out. As Sam and Mickey choreographed it, Big Jim would enter the fight, which would spread like a wildfire throughout the Palace, and become a signature ending carrying two "unconscious" brawlers, one under either arm, up to where Bob Cox's band was playing, calling for a finality to the proceedings. For this, Big Jim needed dialogue and I am proud to say I came up with Big Jim's line to the band, "Play something patriotic," to which Bob and his group would launch into their version of *The Star-Spangled Banner* (w. Francis Scott Key, m. John Stafford Smith) and with the playing of the National Anthem, every brawler would stop, take off their hats and stand at various versions of attention, hands over their hearts.

How to begin the fight on cue? Charles Gray, the wealthy rodeo follower will enter the Palace with Barbara on his arm, with several others, including Mickey Barofsky, as part of his entourage. As Bob Cox's band played for dancing, Steve will make eye contact with Barbara and ask her to dance. Charles Gray will tell Steve, "One dance, Junior." Steve's rodeo rival Bill McKinney, Red Terwiliger, also has eyes for Barbara. When the music slows for Merle Haggard's "Today I Started Loving You Again" (a song I chose), Steve continues for a second dance with Barbara. Enraged, Charles Gray is up. Sensing what is about to happen, Steve will invite McKinney to enjoy a cut in with Barbara.

Sam set the schedule for filming. From about 8:30 to 9:30 each morning, the bar would be open and bartender Dub Taylor (and, I believe, the divorced owner of the Palace, but that is another story!) will serve drinks on the house. Dub had already worked it out where he would stealthily, during the distraction of the fight, be taking money from the cash drawer. By 9 or 9:30, Bob Cox, Rod Hart, and the band were to begin playing for dancing. During this, the choreography of the fight was to begin.

Suddenly, I was called to Steve's Winnebago. Steve was always serious in preparing for his dance scene with Barbara. He got right down to the business of our meeting. He asked, "Why am I called Junior?" I had begun writing the screenplay the previous November. The thought of why Junior was called "Junior" had never crossed my mind! Steve waited patiently for my answer and finally, I admitted "I don't know." He nodded and replied "Okay." Our meeting was over. I had no idea where any of this would go. Steve seemed very pleased with my reply.

With the "half-time" from the rodeo and before Junior must face Sunshine for the second time but now in front of his hometown fans, filming in the Palace began with a Bonner family reunion, initially with Ace, Junior, and Buck Roan (Bob, Steve, and Ben) having a drink at the bar. This was one scene where my writing stood out. I look back on that moment with no firm idea from where the words suddenly arrived, but they did. Ace lifts his shot glass to his mouth, saying before he drinks, "Into the mouth and over the gums (he drinks), look out stomach, here she comes!" He turns to Buck, saying "Lord, but that heals the aches of a loser!" And then he adds, "Buck—if this world is all about winners, then what's for the losers?"

At this point Junior has a reply. But Steve did not like the line I had written. For the second time in twenty-four hours, he asked a direct question of me. This would happen to me a number of times in years to come and I was never prepared for an on-the-spot new line. Ben came to my rescue with a line he must have taken from his many years with John Ford, and it was a beaut: "Somebody's got to hold the horses."

The family reunion suddenly continued as Junior's brother Curly (Joe Don Baker), his wife Ruth (Mary Murphy), their two boys, Ace's squeeze Nurse Arlis (Sandra Deel), and the ex-wife Elvira (Ida Lupino) enter the Palace.

Ace reacts to Junior: "Gentle Jesus, meek and mild, I'm in trouble, son."

Thus begin the moments of the reunion. Ace offers his grandsons a beer and Ruth sharply corrects him with Shirley Temples. Ace sets his grandsons on the bar and toasts them, "To them that's got their roads ahead."

Tension now as Bob Cox's band begins to play for dancing. The initial song "Seven Rings of Silver" was written for composer Jerry Fielding by my good friend David MacKechnie, who had spent time in Nashville as a promising Country music writer. It was a time when poetic writing entered the Nashville world with the presence of Mickey Newbury, Kris Kristofferson, Guy Clark, Willie Nelson, Billy Joe Shaver, and Townes Van Zandt. David was a part of this new Country world of writers. There was wonderful respect from Jerry to David and David to Jerry and David's collaboration with Jerry would continue until Jerry's sudden, untimely death nine years later.

Deserved tension begins because Arlis points out that Ace had devotedly promised her the first dance. Arlis waits. Elvira waits.

Brothers Junior and Curly step in reminding Ace: "Didn't you always save the first dance for Mom?"

Ace admits the two women are a "sweet combination" and he cannot dance with both of them. He chooses Elvira—despite promises to Nurse Arlis. They dance away as Buck swoops in to take Arlis.

This leaves the two brothers to face one another with a reminder of what occurred at the family dinner when Junior power-punched Curly through the window and, the following day at the parade, with Curly's promise to his brother to whip his ass.

Curly knocks his brother down. No double, Steve goes down on his own, after which Curly tells his brother he is trying to keep the family together by offering him a job selling real estate at his retirement Rancheros.

"I'm working on my first million and you're still working on eight seconds," Curly admonishes. But Junior has to go down the rodeo road.

It is a very honest Bonner family moment. The younger brother leaves the door open for Junior, should he change his mind. He and wife Ruth move off to dance.

Meanwhile, rich man Burt, Charles Gray, enters with his entourage. Junior checks out Charmagne.

Thus begins all that Sam and Mickey had set out to do: the fight.

Junior invites Charmagne to dance.

Rich man Burt warns it can be only one dance.

Red (Bill McKinney) wants to cut in, Junior refuses, full attention on Charmagne as the band plays "Today I Started Loving You Again."

With his warning of "Only one dance, Junior" ignored, Burt is up and rushing toward Junior. Wanting no part of this, Junior hands off Red to Charmagne. Burt rushes into Red and Red fights back with a powerful punch knocking Burt backwards.

At Mickey's suggestion, the master shot prior will have everyone dancing in the packed Palace. Sam announces to the crowd, "This is a rehearsal! Let's try it! (My dancing partner, again assigned by Sam, always trying me, was a young woman who serviced him up in his "office" above the Palace.)

When the fight erupted, the master shot in the can, to the complete surprised reactions of the dancers who did not know it was to happen, Sam announced, "That's a print."

So begins a week of fighting. And early morning free drinks to the many extras.

The dog, Dougal, also made his presence known, just as he had in the wild cow-milking, not shy about taking a nip at someone's ass.

During this week, Dorothy and Katherine arrived in Arizona to pick up Stuart from his six weeks at the Orme summer camp. Casey Tibbs recommended I soothe my sore body from punches and falls with a liniment known as Bigeloil, used by horse trainers and banged-up rodeo cowboys. Take a hot bath with Bigeloil. The punctuation on this was Casey, fueled with Champale, ending a scene by giving me one sudden, unexpected punch to my chest, right above the heart. There was no anger from Casey. Like Sam, he was trying me. But, Jesus, it gave worth to a hot bath and Bigeloil!

There were many close cutaway shots of Ace and Elvira and others in the fight. My job was to write these moments into the script for Johnny Franco, the company's script man who was to transpose them daily into the final script. It kept me busy keeping up with Lucien and his crew, and passing on the new scenes to Johnny. (John Franco had worked with Ida before and was a complete professional in one of the most demanding jobs in all of film and television.) One of my jobs was to write the scenes for the coming day's filming and give them to Johnny. Johnny would transcribe them for script continuity, give them to the production office to run off and distribute for the coming day's filming. This was very important to everyone involved to know that day's scenes and schedule.

So one morning, over breakfast with Ben and Casey, they quietly mentioned, "You're in the barrel today." They were smiling.

Just before filming was to begin that morning, as Lucien and the crew were making final preparations, Bob and Ida were out of Makeup (Steve was not working that morning) and all was in place, with all the extras fueled from the bar, with Sam in his director's chair, I was summoned before them all.

My time in the barrel began with: "Where are the fuckin' pages?"

"I typed them up and gave them to Johnny Franco."

"I'm not talking about Johnny Franco, I'm fuckin' talking to you!"

"I typed the pages up. I gave them to the production office to give to Johnny."

"Goddamnit, I'm not talking to Johnny Franco. I'm fuckin' talking to you. Where are the pages?"

If Johnny wanted to let everyone know he had the pages for distribution, he kept a professional silence. And Jim Pratt's production office. Did they fuck up?

"I typed them up, gave them to the production office to run off to give to Johnny."

"I'm fuckin' talking to you! Not Johnny Franco!"

I was not backing down. I repeated, "I typed the pages up, I gave the pages to the production office to give to Johnny."

Was it possible the production office had fucked up?

Silence.

Sam abruptly turned his attention to Lucien and the day's first shot.

I think Sam and John both knew it was exactly as I told it: I had typed the pages. Had the production office not given the pages to Sam? I will never know. Franco never offered an opinion. But he must have given the new pages to Sam and the actors.

My time in the barrel passed.

Sam never acknowledged he had the pages. But he did know I was one who got along well with the actors and the crew, none of whom had ever questioned my professionalism. He also knew Steve was not working that morning. Barbara Leigh had written in her memoir that when Steve arrived, the crew knew who was boss. Would Sam have gone off on me the way he did with Steve there?

Once more, in our time together, Sam tried me.

We moved on with our daily fighting.

Big Jim was not the only local Sam chose. No one who was there will ever forget Curtis, a Native American in his twenties, who cowboy'd on local ranches. Slender of build, Curtis was a drinker, and never without the smile that captured Sam—so much so that he created a scene moment just for him.

As a director, Sam Peckinpah had never directed a contemporary Western. Raised on a ranch near Prescott, Curtis was perhaps in much of the element he had known growing up, just as I was. For years, when he filmed in Monument Valley, John Ford used the Navajos to portray other warlike tribes. Ford knew and respected the Navajos. But Ford's films were period Westerns. *Junior Bonner* may have been among the first, if not the first, to bring in local, real people, to have lines and be very much a part of the storyline.

And with Big Jim and Curtis, we moved into the final moments of our brawl. It was to be a personal moment with Junior and Charmagne as they danced, Steve's question to me and my answer pays off beautifully when, as they improvised, she asks, "Why do they call you, Junior?" and he replies, "I don't know."

As the fight ends with "Play something patriotic" from Big Jim to Bob Cox and his band, and all at attention, hats off, hands over their hearts, we quickly discover another improvisation. This one from Sam. An actress rushes into the women's restroom. Curtis chases after her. In time, when we return to that moment, Curtis, with a big grin, emerges. Big Jim then picks him up and sets him on the bar and pops open a beer for him. "Why," asks Big Jim, is Curtis so intent on chasing the girls?" Curtis drinks and smiles, answering, "Because I like 'em."

In her memoir, *The King, the Queen and The Love Machine*, Barbara Leigh writes her memory of the fight: "The scene [when her dance with Junior is interrupted and the bar wide fight begins] was a little too real for my blood, because everyone was literally smashed by the end. Sam made sure the booze in the glasses was real, not the customary ice tea. Only in a Sam Peckinpah picture could that have happened."

I challenge: No American director has ever captured on screen the real local talent that Sam Peckinpah did in *Junior Bonner*. This was his first contemporary Western-based film. No matter his temperament, the sudden anger, the drinking, sexual behavior, and violence toward the opposite sex, there was no denying his strong empathy toward the people and the town of Prescott, Arizona, and how it showed in the final film.

The brilliance of Sam and Lucien shows in the back stairs scene at the Palace between Bob and Ida and Ace and Elvira. Similar to the strong father-son scene at the depot, here was the moment of love lost and perhaps to be regained between Ace Bonner, the dreamer bound for Australia, and Elvira Bonner, her future bound to her son's Reata Rancheros gift shop.

The scene began inside the Palace. The crowd is gathered around Ace. Elvira stands in the background. One of those Sam wanted close to Ace was Roy, the Alex he had cast with Bob, together just before the parade. Alex was now known to all of us as Roy. To Sam the reality of Roy with Ace at the bar was a necessary punctuation to the moment he had created earlier between the two of them.

But where is Roy? Clearly the recently retired real cowboy knew nothing of the scene or his part in it. Sam was adamant Roy must be standing with Ace at the bar. Somehow, those dispatched to find our Roy, found him and the scene could begin. To me, even all these years later, this was Sam Peckinpah at his finest.

Ace stands at the bar, proudly reminding himself of his glory days meeting Jack Dempsey in his Manhattan restaurant "as one champ to another" during the Madison Square Garden Rodeo, the challenge to ride a bull named Holy Joe. As Ace tells it, "I rode that bull and after eight seconds there was eighteen thousand big city dudes on their feet, with my name on their lips." Emotionally filled with the moment, he adds, "That was the last time, though." All the while, Elvira listens to the story, clearly having heard it before, and she turns away to leave out the back door of the Palace.

It had been raining. Glimpses of sunlight now and then shone through the dark skies.

Could we steal enough time between the rain to film this important scene? Lucien Ballard lit the scene. We had to hurry.

Inside the Palace, Ace turns. He hurries outside after her. He needs to talk to her. "By hook or crook I'm goin' to Australia." And so the scene unfolds on the back stairs, leading up to rooms upstairs. Ace is a spoken example of lamenting changing times—no more silver, no more bounty on the lions.

He has the idea she could go to Australia with him. As far as she is concerned, he is no more than a broken record and he can go to hell or Australia, and with a smile, he reminds her they are both down under. "Dreams and sweet talk—that's all you are," she comes back at him, and he is quick to ask that she stay with him that night and he will sweeten the dreams—"Remember?" and she slaps him.

"Sure as hell, I had that coming," he admits. "You sure as hell did," she replies.

He is leaving. She knows it. "Then all we have left is tonight?" she asks.

This is their moment. "Anyway, Ellie…if you've seen one rodeo, you've seen 'em all," he tells her for they will not be going out to the rodeo grounds to see Junior and Sunshine; they will be together for the last time. They go up the stairs together.

Wisely, Sam deleted a moment I had written where Buck and Arlis were already in a room upstairs watching this unfold. Arlis had lost her Ace but gained her Buck.

Andrew Antoniades and Mike Siegel write in their book, *Steve McQueen: The Actor and His Films*: "The scene on the staircase between Lupino and Preston is one of the best in the film. Filmed by one of America's leading directors who proved he could handle action and drama equally well."

In her interview with Garner Simmons for his book on Sam, Ida confessed that after the scene, Sam came to her and she asked how the scene went. "Lousy," he replied. When he saw the look on Ida's face, he grinned and gave her a big hug; for the tears he shed at the rehearsal table were now a reality.

I often think of how I came to write the scene.

I think I know.

When I came home to tell Dorothy that Joe Wizan wanted me to write this for Steve McQueen, I surely was the dreamer.

Floyd Baze, whose professional career in rodeo had been made by challenging bull and broncs, was chosen by Mickey to double for Steve in riding the big black bull named Sunshine. Sam chose not to film each individual bull ride leading up to Junior and Sunshine, but to edit each bull ride one after the other and then to the final moment.

To me, Baze's ride on Sunshine is one of the more incredible stunts ever put on film. True, the stopwatch seems to go on a very long eight seconds while intercutting the ride, but the ride itself is damn well dangerously exciting.

Junior rides Sunshine and the success gives him the winning score for the Frontier Days Rodeo in front of his hometown people.

The first place prize money belongs to him. The exclamation point to this is the rodeo clown jumping into his arms; Red Terwiliger, Junior's rival, knowing he has been beaten out; and Charmagne, so proud of the cowboy who will soon enough be on his way to the next rodeo.

The filming was nearly complete. But "overtime" was not up.

An iconic photo of Steve McQueen shows him behind the chutes during the production of Junior Bonner, but the "Marlboro Man" look is out of character for Junior Bonner, who carried his own makings and rolled his own cigarettes.
Rosebrook Family Collection.

Barbara Leigh, McQueen, and Sam Peckinpah strode across the rodeo arena during production of Junior Bonner. *The Frontier Days Rodeo Committee's accommodation of the film crew's needs during the live competitions gave the picture an authenticity rarely seen in rodeo movies.* Rosebrook Family Archive.

After the conclusion of the Frontier Days' Rodeo week, Yavapai County Fairgrounds hosts horse-racing through the summer. Peckinpah enjoyed holding production meetings about the rodeo action in a front-row box while the horses raced. Back Row l.-r.: Katy Haber (standing), Jeb Rosebrook; Front Row: Don "Red" Barry, Peckinpah, Frank Kowalski, and two unknown fairground officials. Mike Siegel Collection.

The film company used a VIP grandstand across from the main stands to do close-up cutaways of the principal cast members and fans watching the rodeo. In the foreground, Ida Lupino (leaning against the railing), Don "Red" Barry, and Sandra Deel enjoy a moment in the shade as the crew sets up for the next shot. Mike Siegel Collection.

The off-screen romance of Barbara Leigh and Steve McQueen (shown with an unknown crew member) created on-screen chemistry between their characters.
Courtesy Barbara Leigh.

From day one of pre-production to the end of the film's post-production, Katy Haber (foreground, walking backwards, listening to and leading Peckinpah and McQueen through the crowd) was the director's primary assistant on and off the set. Mike Siegel Collection.

Two of Peckinpah's closest friends and members of his famous "Peckinpah Company," property master Bobby Visiglia and assistant director Frank Kowalski, were key to the production of Junior Bonner, *despite the fact that Kowalski got fed up with Peckinpah and returned to L.A. before the end of principal photography.* Mike Siegel Collection.

Peckinpah directed his crew to start pouring drinks every morning at nine during the week of filming at the Palace Bar to prime the participants in the dance and fight scenes. Rosebrook Family Collection.

The two primary locations of the Junior Bonner *script were the Yavapai County Fairgrounds and the Palace Bar on Whiskey Row (Montezuma Street). Peckinpah, caught in a moment of quiet contemplation next to his son Matthew (as Tim Bonner, Curly's son) during the production of the pre-dance family-at-the-bar reconciliation sequence, liked the Palace so much he made it his secondary production headquarters, renting a room on the second floor. Mary Murphy can be seen directly in the background.* Mike Siegel Collection.

Three of Junior Bonner's *iconic leading men—Robert Preston, McQueen, and Ben Johnson—enjoyed a congenial moment together at the Palace Bar during production.* Mike Siegel Collection.

In addition to an open bar, Peckinpah's dance and bar fight sequences in the Palace Bar were primed with the live music of the Palace's house band, led by Bob Cox with Rod Hart (credited songwriter and vocalist of "Rodeo Man" *and* "Arizona Morning"*). The dance and fight scenes included Peckinpah (in a cameo) cast members, crew members (including screenwriter Rosebrook, his tennis shoes and white pants can be seen sticking out from the bandstand), and local extras.* Rosebrook Family Collection.

Unbeknownst to the audience, McQueen and Leigh's memorable moment in the phone booth during the Palace Bar fight scene intimated their own off-camera, personal relationship. Rosebrook Family Collection.

Miller High Life beer, a sponsor of the film (the distributor donated hundreds of cases to the crew) received highly visible product placement in Junior Bonner, *including by McQueen just before Curly reminds his brother that he's working on his first million and "you're still working on eight seconds."* Rosebrook Family Collection.

Preston and Lupino's temporary reconciliation of their on-screen relationship as Ace and Elvira Bonner begins during the dance and fight sequence inside the Palace, and concludes in their scene on the bar's back stairs.
Close-up of Robert Preston and Ida Lupino, Courtesy Rosebrook Family Collection/
Robert Preston and Ida Lupino Dancing, Courtesy Jeff Slater Collection.

Prior to filming the dance scene between McQueen and Leigh, in which Charmagne's character asks Junior how he got his name, McQueen asked the screenwriter Rosebrook, "Why am I called Junior?" His answer: "I don't know." And that is what McQueen replied when Leigh asked her during the dance— pure McQueen movie magic. Rosebrook Family Collection.

Stuntman Floyd Baze doubled for McQueen during his rodeo action sequences, including his winning ride on the notorious bull, Sunshine.
Rosebrook Family Collection.

McQueen's character Junior visits the bull pens behind the rodeo arena to confront his fears—and nemesis—Sunshine the Bull (off-camera), before he rides him to victory in front on his hometown fans. Jeff Slater Collection.

McQueen, known for doing many of his stunts during his television and movie career, did not ride any bulls out of the chute, but he prepped with the company's in-house world champion, rodeo consultant Casey Tibbs, on how to properly prepare on screen for his rides as rodeo star Junior Bonner.
Rosebrook Family Collection.

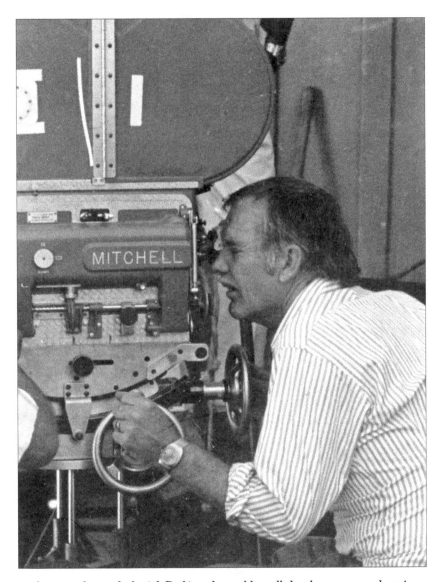

Anyone who worked with Peckinpah would recall that he was never happier than when on location, on-set, and behind the camera. Mike Siegel Collection.

In 1971, Lupino and Preston had been professionally acting since 1931 and 1938, respectively, when they played opposite each other in Junior Bonner, *a magical casting of two pros whose performances nearly steal the movie from McQueen.* Mike Siegel Collection.

Despite his well-known volatility on and off the set, one of Peckinpah's greatest strengths as a director was his ability to work intimately with his actors in rehearsals in preparation for the action on the set. His work with Lupino and Preston, and their final scene together in Junior Bonner, *is considered one of his best ever directed scenes.* Mike Siegel Collection.

The Junior Bonner *production company took over the alley behind Whiskey Row to stage the boom shot that Peckinpah needed to film the concluding farewell scene between Lupino and Preston.* Mike Siegel Collection.

Peckinpah, a renowned writer himself, had screenwriter Rosebrook with him nearby, on set, from the beginning to the end of production, including during the scene between Lupino and Preston behind the Palace, which he shot just as it was written. Mike Siegel Collection.

A regular and loyal member of the Peckinpah Company, Chalo Gonzalez—who joined the crew mid-production, and was paid by Peckinpah to be a location assistant—enjoyed a fun moment with Preston. Mike Siegel Collection.

Peckinpah depended on Katy Haber to keep him on track throughout the production of Junior Bonner, *especially since they had such a short turn-around from post-production of* Straw Dogs *(1971) to pre-production and production of the film completely on location in Prescott and Yavapai County—in coordination with the live events of the Frontier Days Rodeo and Parade.* Mike Siegel Collection.

The majority of the scenes starring McQueen in the arena, including when he is bucked off during the saddle-bronc sequence, and his winning ride on Sunshine, were filmed after the conclusion of the rodeo and when the horses weren't running at Prescott Downs. Mike Siegel Collection.

One of Joe Wizan and Peckinpah's biggest challenges as producer and director of Junior Bonner *was staging their film crew in the arena amidst the live action of the Prescott Rodeo.* Mike Siegel Collection.

McQueen always tried to push his stunt work to the edge of his ability for realism in his films. He did ride out of the chute for the saddle-bronc sequence, but let a stunt man finish the ride and get bucked off. Just before McQueen rode out of the chute on the bronc, he mistakenly goosed the stunt horse with his spurs, which resulted in an unscripted scene between the star and the horse that is included in the final cut, adding a true moment of realism and spontaneity in the rodeo action. Mike Siegel Collection.

The rodeo action scenes with McQueen, including the saddle bronc sequence in which he is bucked off, were filmed in the afternoon to maintain the continuity between the first and second acts of the rodeo, and the dance, bar fight and, reconciliation scenes at the Palace. Mike Siegel Collection.

ACT THREE

During the Palace fight scene, one of the most important elements was the music played from the bandstand by Bob Cox and his band, with duets on Merle Haggard's "Today I Started Loving You Again" sung by Bob and singer/picker Rod Hart. They also sang two original songs, music and lyrics by Rod Hart. One with an upbeat rockabilly beat was "Rodeo Man" and the other, a Jimmy Webb-style ballad, "Arizona Morning." "Rodeo Man" was played just before the fight broke out, and the dance floor was rocking away with the Prescott extras, fueled with free drinks and having the Fourth of July time of their lives. Particularly adept was the large presence of Curly (Joe Don Baker) and wife Ruth (Mary Murphy).

Both songs were presented to Sam and Joe early in the filming when, due to costs, Buck Owens and the Buckaroos had been ruled out.

But now as filming was nearly finished and our time in Prescott ending, a decision had to be made for songs. Joe Wizan was considering the idea of creatively adding both "Rodeo Man" and "Arizona Morning" on screen to the film, incorporating them into the final score Jerry Fielding was going to write. Alex Taylor, James Taylor's brother, had already been negotiated to perform the title song for Capricorn Records

Alex Taylor had his brother's name, although not the fame, yet he was with Capricorn Records and to sing the opening title song to a McQueen/Peckinpah film would certainly add a positive move in his career. Far from the glamour of the rock world were two Prescott musicians with two songs composed for the film. "Rodeo Man" was a no-brainer to be included in the film. But the Jimmy Webb-style of "Arizona Morning?" Joe Wizan was intrigued.

The decision was deferred.

With filming nearly complete, Joe Wizan had suddenly vanished. He was bound for Calgary to prepare for his next picture, *Prime*

Cut (1972), directed by Michael Ritchie and starring Lee Marvin, Gene Hackman with Sissy Spacek.

Joe left his responsibilities to Mickey Barofsky.

Sam took to reminding all that our producer, Joe Wizan, had better things to do. In fact, Sam relished Joe's departure, reminding us Joe was an opportunist who, having spent all the time he could with us, now had better things to do in Calgary. In his way, Sam was reminding me that Joe charged Marty Baum $100,000 for the screenplay and paid me half that amount and kept fifty-grand for himself.

Before he left, Joe mentioned he wanted to do another film with me. He wanted a period Western along the lines of his favorite all-time Western, *Shane* (1953). It was to be written for Steve and Sam. We two would work on the story in Calgary.

Away "the Wizard of Wizan," as I would come to call him, went to Canada.

And for Sam, Steve, and all, Joe was not missed. We had final work to do.

Sam had thoughts about the ending. For me it had all been inspired by my visit to the rodeo and Prescott the previous year. The dancers, rockabilly and Country being played live, and the young woman who danced past me with one word: "Smile." These were local ranch people as well as those up from Phoenix, looking for a time out of time in their nine-to-five lives, and—to use a term from some years later—in this time of sexual revolution, a "hook up."

To me, none of this was new, save it being 1970 in Prescott and not the fifties when I was part of the Pow Wow Fourth of July scene in Flagstaff where Native Americans, mainly Navajo, gathered for a pow wow celebration of a rodeo, a parade, jewelry sales, and, among the men, an appetite for strong drink; while we whites danced and drank at The Museum Club. For many of us, it was time out of time, finding a young woman to drink and dance with, and maybe more, if the gods smiled upon us.

My ending for *Junior Bonner* was based on those experiences where a weekend often could be "Hello" and "Good-bye." So it was Charmagne, the young woman from Phoenix who found time out of time with Junior. They part in the sunlight of a Prescott morning beside her Volkswagen Beetle before he heads for Salinas and she back to her nine-to-five gig in a Phoenix bank.

Sam creatively worked it out visually and Junior fit into it all. First Junior would take Charmagne, not to her Volkswagen Bug, but to the airport for a flight home to Phoenix.

Secondly, he will drive to his mother's. As he does, he will pass the Palace, where Ace and his dog Dougal are just coming out onto the street. Seeing Junior drive by, Ace runs down the sidewalk shouting to get Junior's attention. Not seeing him or hearing him, Junior drives on. Junior arrives at his mother's. He knocks on the door. But no one answers. Junior turns to leave. His mother calls his name. He turns. Elvira is framed behind the screen door. "You had to win," she tells him. And Junior has that long good-bye beat with his mother before returning to his Cadillac. It is almost the final family moment. Not quite.

Finally, Junior arrived at the travel agency. Sam and Lucien framed it so we see Buck Roan's trucks, carrying the broncs and the bulls, leaving Prescott on their way to the next rodeo, presumably Salinas. Junior buys a one-way airline ticket to Australia for "a man and his dog." And "Make it first class." Junior pays. He asks it be delivered to Ace Bonner at the Palace. As he turns to exit, the woman travel agent asks who is sending this to Ace Bonner? With that one-and-only almost-shy Steve McQueen grin, Junior replies, "Tell him Junior sent you."

Dramatically, in the editing, Sam had all these final moments ending in a freeze frame.

Seeing it for the first time, these moments brought tears to my eyes. Months before, these were my moments arriving to paper from my dad's 1948 Royal portable typewriter, then with Sam, creatively working them out to be put into place on the same typewriter. Sam Peckinpah, known as "The Master of Violence" in his visual, creative, emotional mind, had met a family named Bonner in the town of Prescott, Arizona.

He will return to violence. He and Steve will never again meet the Bonner family. But neither will ever forget them.

There suddenly arose a true emergency before the film could be completed. Due to a sudden outbreak in Yavapai County of equine encephalitis—a virus affecting horses spread by infected mosquitoes from birds and small mammals that causes inflammation and swelling of the brain that begins four-to-eight days after the mosquito bite—the county authorities enacted a law prohibiting the moving of any horses from one place to another.

What to do? We had yet to film Junior leaving town with his Cadillac pulling the horse trailer—with, of course, his horse in it. Legally, the horse could not be moved. What to do?

Too many years have passed for me to remember exactly who solved the problem. But if I had to guess, it may well have been our indispensable prop man, Bobby Vasiglia.

Beside the Palace was a Western wear store. Hanging above the store as an advertisement was a life-sized model horse. If it was Bobby, he had the idea to borrow the horse; take it down, paint it the color of Junior's horse, place it in the trailer and drive out of town. The Western wear store agreed. The model horse came down, was temporarily re-painted, and into Junior's trailer it went. Audiences seeing the movie never knew that what they saw was not a real horse but a model horse that hangs above a retail store on Whiskey Row.

This gives evidence to not only the quick thinking of Bobby and our crew, but to the cooperation of the people and the merchants of Prescott.

The final day of filming arrived. August 17, 1971. The day was overcast, humid with an ominous thunderstorm forming over the seven thousand feet of Mingus Mountain to the east. This was to be part of the opening of the film with Junior driving into Prescott, and the impending thunderstorm making its presence felt. We were to drive on Highway 89A eastward toward the once-populated copper mining town of Jerome, now a semi-tourist ghost town curiosity, literally perched on the side of Mingus, with the reputation of sliding so many inches a year. Historically, according to *Arizona Place Names*, copper was discovered there by the Spanish as early as 1582. At the height of its copper mining boom, Jerome had been home to a population of 15,000.

I rode in Steve's pickup, sitting between Steve, who was driving, and Sam. One of the teamsters was in charge of Junior's Cadillac.

Steve pulled over beside the highway and stopped. He said he had to take a leak. It is more than possible he also needed to smoke a joint. He got out, walked out toward the mesquite and ranch grass.

As Steve disappeared within the mesquite, Sam came around to the driver's side, got in, shut the door and started the engine. We drove off....

Holy shit!

We just ditched the world's highest-paid movie star, leaving him alone amidst a foreign land of mesquite and range grass, with his dick in his hands and a joint in his mouth.

"Sam?" I asked. Sam smiled, saying nothing.

Remembering when Steve took Sam and me on a furiously fast ride in his pickup when looking for locations prior to filming, a ride that took at high speed sharp curves and turns, knowing Sam, I believe this was perhaps payback time.

Sam did not seem to have any intention of turning around. We followed behind the film crew and Junior's Cadillac.

Ahead was Mingus Mountain. The sky was turning darker.

Finally, we stopped for filming.

I waited. Sam turned around.

We had come at least four miles. The land looked all the same.

There was no sign of Steve McQueen.

Then, beneath an ever-darkening sky, there he was, on the other side of us, hitchhiking.

Sam stopped, did a U-turn and picked up Steve. I sat in the middle between them, silently cringing, as Sam drove, and neither spoke. If Steve had caused Sam problems—like holding up a half a day's filming with Ida and the apple pie, or causing the painful delay in rehearsing the railroad depot scene with Bob—and Sam, sensing Barbara Leigh was correct in saying the crew knew when Steve was there he was "the boss," as well as the scary drive in this same pickup while supposedly looking for locations, it was the more than the mischievous side of a Peckinpah payback as to who was really the boss.

We filmed. Thunder and lightning and rain arrived. Steve raised the top of the old Cadillac convertible. This will become a part of the opening credits.

The sun came out. The entire crew ended up in a Jerome saloon. I stood beside Steve at the bar. Like many movie stars, he had no cash on him, despite those six-figure checks Bill Pierce told me about, and he needed a beer. I paid. Small talk. We drank together.

Looking out at the pool table in the Palace one day several weeks before, I mentioned I was probably the worst player in America. Sam boasted he was the worst player in North America, which included an actor who played a Mexican general in *The Wild Bunch*.

Somehow it was decided on a challenge by one of us, to play it off, two games out of three. Only the rules were that to be the winner was to lose the game! And to drink with each missed shot. I forget what Sam was drinking. I was into Old Forester bourbon.

Sam's brother-in-law, Walter Peter, a tall, very muscular stock trader in Los Angeles and his sister, Fern Lea, arrived to be with Sam as filming ended. It was an uproarious time between Sam and me, with, by the second game, pool balls bouncing off the table, crashing around the floor, even once or more, out to the sidewalk.

Tomorrow we were all leaving Prescott.

My ride home to North Hollywood was with First Assistant Director Mack Harding. Following the pool game, I went outside to a payphone, calling Dorothy to tell her of my homecoming plans with Mack. As we talked, I looked up to see a smiling Sam. He wanted the last word with Dorothy.

"Jeb's not coming home right away," he told her. "He's going with me to research brothels in Nevada."

If I agreed? Is this true? I told her again I was for sure coming home.

Still smiling, pleased as Lucifer with his offer, Sam went off for dinner with Walter and Fern Lea.

Our pool competition had ended in a draw.

Perhaps as well, our relationship.

In his 2014 memoir, *Goin' Crazy with Sam Peckinpah*, Max Evans writes: "Over time Sam began to accept Jeb."

That evening, packed and ready for tomorrow, I was spending my last night at the Prescottonian. It was a ghost of what it had been over the past ten weeks. Sandra Deel, Dub Taylor, Ben, Barbara, Bob, and Ida were all gone. Would I ever see them again?

Casey was among the last to exit. Casey, who had spent the summer weeks down the second-floor hall from me, had stopped by while I was gone. We had become close friends during the filming. I had been his foil when his French lady friend, Renee, from Hollywood called his room while he was involved with one of our extras.

"If she calls your room, tell her I was here," he advised. No one in Prescott would forget his movie rooster that earned forty dollars a day or, during a break in our Palace fighting, when he went next door to the barbershop and, offering his services as a barber, gave a customer, grateful to being serviced by Casey Tibbs, a haircut that was near bald on the sides and lawn-mowered on top. In honor of our friendship, Possibly America's Most Beloved Cowboy, left the one condom he had not used atop my suitcase.

Just before falling asleep, I heard shouting and cursing from the café at the foot of the motel's entrance. I was up. I pulled on my Levi's, and in bare feet, headed to the parking lot. The sound of police sirens echoed the night coming toward the café. As I arrived at the café, Sam's brother-in-law, Walter, was damn near carrying Sam out of the café, shoving him into a station wagon. A bottle, belonging to one of them, fell to the pavement, shattering into pieces.

Standing there, bare feet fortunately not hit by the glass, I watched the station wagon swerve out of the parking lot, speeding off, passing the oncoming police, sirens wailing.

What happened? I asked someone coming out of the café. I learned that a local realtor had, in effect, told Sam he wasn't as hot shit as he thought he was. Sam reacted and hit him, and the fight was on. Someone called the police. Walter moved into action and literally carried Sam to his getaway station wagon. A bottle fell en route.

Walter whipped a U-turn, heading away, passing sirens and lights as he sped the escape.

For a time, I stared down at broken glass and the pool of booze.

And so it was Sam Peckinpah who made sure the reputation he arrived with in Prescott remained undamaged as he left town.

I turned and, in my bare feet, went back to the Prescottonian for my last night in town.

No one had tied a tin can to my ass and mailed me home.

***

We left Prescott behind. There were some in the crew who discovered mutual relationships with the young and available women of the town. A young woman will learn film crews are gypsies, coming to a location for weeks, even months, becoming a part of wherever their work takes them. Married or single, their hormones accompany them. This is hardly anything new. In William Wellman, Jr.'s excellent biography of his father, director William ("Wild Bill") Wellman, his father recounts when he directed the silent classic, *Wings* (1927) in San Antonio, there was additionally, a second film company working there. It seems, between the two film companies, the female elevator operators at the hotels where the crews stayed, gave birth nine months later.

For the first time since I had chosen to change my career as of January 1, 1968, the Rosebrook family had money: $45,000 cash. We had paid off Dorothy's mother, Eunice, for the loan on our Plymouth station wagon. Through my old Orme School friend, Merle Frost, who was in the business of leasing cars, I leased a dark blue, sporty new Camaro. Dorothy had thoughts of possibly moving from our small North Hollywood home, following the many who left the area for newer homes farther west, Woodland Hills being the most popular.

My dad, who had informed me when I chose to change careers, that an elevator operator in New York made more money than I did, was now much relieved. And proud.

Good things were also happening to my good friend and mentor, Earl Hamner, Jr. His most recent novel, *The Homecoming: A Christmas Story* (CBS, 1971), set in Depression-era Virginia, was to be filmed for CBS by newly formed Lorimar Productions. The new company was well-funded by Las Vegas based Merv Adelson. Like its predecessor, *Spencer's Mountain, The Homecoming* was to be filmed in Wyoming.

Upon returning home, my first assignment from Sam, now deeply involved in editing, was to write "wild lines" to create background dialogue between rodeo contestants behind the chutes, etc. This was extensive work as there were so many rodeo scenes with banter among cowboys around and behind the chutes or where calf ropers and bull doggers, and barrel racers readied themselves for their events. This dialogue was to replace the often jumbled small talk in the background of the real moments. It would then be recorded by what in Hollywood is known as The Loop Group, specialists in adding such incidental dialogue. In addition to beginning to edit *Junior Bonner*, Sam was involved in putting the final edits on the soon-to-be-released *Straw Dogs*. Lead editor, Englishman Roger Spottiswoode, had spent time in Prescott during the summer, which divided Sam between a picture being filmed and another working toward the final product.

Steve was also back home, and in the middle of a divorce. He was still seeing Barbara, who was also back in L.A. The press had reported Steve's next project was to be the lead in Paramount's *The Great Gatsby* (1974). Married to Paramount's chief executive, Robert Evans, Ali MacGraw was on board to play Daisy. Peter Bogdanovich was signed to direct.

Steve was still very much on Barbara's mind. She wrote in her memoir with Marshall Terrill, *The King, McQueen and The Love Machine*: "Things between me and Steve were great. I was really starting to like this bad boy." (Elvis became aware of Steve when she had to admit their relationship to the King when he wanted to visit her in Prescott. "I always wanted to see a real cowboy town," he'd lamented.)

But everything was about to change. Bogdanovich bowed out of *Gatsby* to direct *What's Up, Doc?* (1972), Steve's friend and one-time publicist, David Foster, was setting up to produce *The Getaway* (1972), a crime caper with a screenplay by Walter Hill, adapted from a novel by Jim Thompson. Steve joined his friend for the lead on *The Getaway*. Steve and David agreed Sam was perfect for the project. Both Steve and Sam, I believe, were anxious to return to what made them successful: Steve in action paired with Sam's penchant for violence.

After getting along relatively well in Prescott, they appeared to be the perfect duo for *The Getaway*.

They needed a leading lady for Steve. With the delay on *Gatsby*, the trio set their sights on Ali MacGraw, who had, as I heard, turned down the script. None of the trio were ready to admit her refusal. Rewrite for the female lead. Try again. Do not give up.

Although I did not know it, this was to be the last time I saw Steve. I stopped by their production office to drop off some of the wild lines of dialogue for Sam. Steve was there, surprised to see me. "I thought you lived in Arizona?" he said. I explained I lived in North Hollywood. Always affable and friendly to me, it was clear he had quickly put "Junior" in the rearview mirror and was fast moving on. Using Sam for *The Getaway*, I'm sure, in his mind, was a vehicle for the commercial success he was accustomed to earning. As to having his way, I'm sure he was also mindful of what Barbara had noted on the subject. When Steve showed up on the set, the crew knew he was the boss.

What struck me was Steve's voice. It was unusually husky, with a tone of rasp to it. Too much smoking or the weed, I thought at the time. It turned out I was right. Near the end of *The Getaway*, Steve was taken to the hospital to have some polyps removed. Doctors told him to quit smoking. As for Sam, he was on the glide path to the release of *Straw Dogs*, editing *Junior Bonner*, and prepping *The Getaway*. He was in the prime of his career.

I was also on a new creative journey. Via Mike Wise and CMA, I signed my new contract with Joe Wizan and was off to work out the storyline for our next collaboration—the period Western he envisioned for Steve and Sam. Joe flew me to Calgary, where filming on *Prime Cut* was set to begin. Unfortunately, in the midst of our story collaboration, Joe received a phone call changing everything for the time being: his dad had suffered a heart attack in Los Angeles. Tickets were made for us to fly that night to Vancouver and then on to Los Angeles. Joe still had no car. I arranged for Dorothy to meet us at LAX and from there whisk us to the hospital.

As we left to change planes in Vancouver, the ever-confident Joe gave his card to the flight attendant with a smile and an invitation to give him a call.

Jerry Fielding had been signed to compose the score. I had been through the entire process so far, in the making of a motion picture, beginning with the original story and screenplay, typed out on my dad's 1948 Royal portable. Now it was to score the film.

While I did not know it at the time, for I only knew Jerry's reputation for his brilliant score for *The Wild Bunch*, I was meeting a true genius of his generation. He was now fifty years old. Born Joshua Itzhak Feldman in Pittsburgh, he made his way, following illness and a brief stay at the Carnegie Institute for Instrumentalists as a young man, up through the big band era (an arranger for Tommy Dorsey and Les Brown among others), surviving being blacklisted, a change of professional name to Jerry Fielding, and, after radio and television, brought into film composing by Otto Preminger with *Advise and Consent* (1962).

I had many mentors on my *Junior Bonner* journey, and now it was Jerry and music. Additionally, Joe, with Jerry and Marty Baum, had to make a decision on "Arizona Morning," the lead song Rod Hart had written and composed and presented to Wizan during the summer when there was to be no Buck Owens playing in the Palace scenes.

We all knew the value of "Rodeo Man" as it was played during the fight. The tape of "Arizona Morning" was truly haunting and beautiful.

"What do you think? For the main title?" Joe questioned. I felt it was perfect.

There was a serious complication. Rising rock star, Alex Taylor, twenty-four, the older brother of James Taylor, had been signed by Capricorn Records, and a title song for the film had been composed and was to now be recorded by Alex.

If Joe chose "Arizona Morning," what about Alex Taylor?

Meanwhile, Jerry invited me to join him during the scoring of the film. He conducted a full orchestra. Added to this was steel-guitar-player Red Rhodes and the popular bluegrass group, the Dillards. To get the effect of the rodeo parade with the Luke Air Force Band, their John Phillips Souza music was dubbed over by Jerry's symphony—he took them outside between two sound stages, so that the marching music echoed off the two walls. The individual scenes were shown in black and white. Jerry's orchestra played, from his composition, to each scene. Red Rhodes and the Dillards, unable to read music, more or less freelanced under Jerry's direction.

For me to be included in this process was an honor. I have no idea how many writers of an original screenplay go on location for the entire shoot, much less follow the process through to the film score with a full orchestra, but for me, it was the gift of being made aware of just how important a score is to every moment in every scene. Oftentimes it may be hardly noticed, a low-key emphasis playing beneath drama or humor. Many of the rodeo scenes were emphasized beautifully and simply with the bluegrass Dillards and/or Red Rhodes and his steel guitar.

During this time Jerry and his wife, Camille, invited Dorothy and me to their home to listen to the score in progress. I remember telling Jerry I could have written the script to his score. He also played his completed score to the period Western, *Chato's Land* (1972), starring Charles Bronson and directed by Michael Winner. Jerry had been through the highs and lows of a high torn down by being blacklisted and then discovering his gift for composing film scores. At age fifty, he was at the height of his talent.

But what about the opening song? Alex Taylor came by during the scoring to record the Dennis Lambert and Brian Potter song "Bound to be Back Again," a blend of rock and Country by a hot song-writing duo recently signed to ABC-Dunhill with a major hit "One Tin Soldier," among many. At twenty-five, Alex Taylor, having landed his first recording contract, was very full of himself, arriving with his entourage, filled with a mix of joints and booze.

What Alex Taylor did not know was that Joe Wizan had flown Rod Hart over to record "Arizona Morning." Rod was awaiting his turn in an adjacent room. When Alex left with his merry band of rockers (and stoners) in tow, Rod entered.

This was damn sure one helluva long ways from the Palace!

"Sing your ass off, Rod," we told him.

And he did. Backed by Jerry's orchestra he began, "Arizona Morning," with a flawless beautiful performance. We were all thrilled.

We knew right then what Alex Taylor did not know. Rod Hart and "Arizona Morning" would be the title song for *Junior Bonner*.

Steve, Sam, and producer David Foster had finally accomplished their mission. They lured Ali MacGraw for the female lead in *The Getaway*. They went on their way to Texas for the filming. I went to work with Joe on a new screenplay, with the working title of *Jack Ballard*. Joe had completed *Prime Cut*, and was in the midst of a NASCAR racing picture called *The Last American Hero* with Jeff Bridges, and directed by Lamont Johnson.

Screenings of *Junior Bonner* were held at the home of CMA's head man, Freddie Fields. A Hollywood columnist who was at the Steve McQueen screening wrote that it was one of Steve's finest-ever performances. *Los Angeles Herald Examiner* film critic Win Blevins attended the Joe Wizan screening. He recalled that when the film ended, Joe turned to a Who's Who of directors, including Francis Ford Coppola, and asked, "What do you think?" According to Blevins, none replied and silently left.

To this day Win Blevins cannot explain the silence. My thought is that Sam had made a non-violent film with beautiful performances from all. How to explain that?

Meanwhile, two rodeo films were out and on the way out. First was Cliff Robertson's *JW Coop* (1971), which he starred in, directed, and co-wrote with Gary Cartwright and Bud Shrake. Like *Junior Bonner*, Robertson went on location and filmed the majority of the picture in McAlester, Oklahoma, and Springville, California. Ironically, the same year that *Junior Bonner* was in production, my agent, with CMA, Mike Wise, had helped broker another rodeo picture, starring Jim Coburn titled *The Honkers* (1972), a modestly budgeted film shot in New Mexico with Slim Pickens and Lois Nettleton, written by Steve Tennant (also the director) and multi-talented Steven Lodge (writer, director, costumer, costume designer, actor, and stunt man).

Coburn was working, but no sign of *Ward Craft*. It seemed to be increasingly clear financing for the film might have to come from independent sources rather than via the studio system. If it were to be made at all, director Paul Mielche had polished my script to his satisfaction. A window of time had to be found in Coburn's schedule.

Steve McQueen had incredible instincts, followed not far behind by Jeb Rosebrook. Steve went public in a taped interview that *Junior Bonner* was an art house film and should open slowly, market by market. My instinct was that it should not be advertised as a rodeo film but as a family in the midst of contemporary change with Steve as the centerpiece.

Junior Bonner was marketed as a rodeo film, and to open in June 1972 at the Grauman's Chinese Theater in Hollywood. So much for Steve and Jeb's two bits.

A test screening was to be held in April in El Paso, where Sam and Steve were headquartered filming *The Getaway*. By now the gossip columns were filled with more than rumors of the romance between Steve and Ali MacGraw, leaving her husband, Robert Evans, and his studio and *The Great Gatsby* on the sidelines. In time, Steve will break the ties with Barbara, devoting time to a future with Ali MacGraw. (For Barbara, there was still Elvis and MGM president Jim Aubrey).

The premier was held at Grauman's Chinese Theater in June. When the names of those connected with the making of the film were mentioned from on stage prior to the showing, Dorothy recalls that, although my name was included in the program, it was not mentioned in the introductions. When the showing ended, a voice behind us said, "That was a goddamn poem." I turned to look. It was Warren Oates.

The reviews were mixed, although most were positive. Penelope Gilliant in *The New Yorker* mentioned that the script had the feeling of Tennessee Williams to it, while another called me "Tennessee Williams in chaps." Warren Oates took issue with Jay Cocks of *Time* magazine who, the day of the premier, in his review, took issue with the ending and Sam, indicating it was a failure of Peckinpah ideology that the hero did not stand up at the end to be a definition of values put forth in *Ride the High Country*, *The Ballad of Cable Hogue*, and, most especially, *The Wild Bunch*, because Steve drove away to let his home country be plowed under. No one, to my knowledge, these years later, praised Sam for capturing a slice of hometown America circa 1971, and the changes therein occurring.

The Wild Bunch put up a fight in their era of change and paid the price, to a man.

Joel McCrea and Randolph Scott gave up their lives unto their values in *Ride the High Country*; Jason Robards, in his dying moments, literally on his deathbed, gave an eloquent eulogy to the passing of the West, yet Junior drove away with the simple line to Charmagne, "Gotta go down my own road."

Audiences wanted Steve in action. More than a bull named Sunshine. Critics and audiences seemed very much the same about Sam, wanting the violence which was on its way to creating his talent known as "The Master of Violence."

Despite the echoes of praise from more critics than not, *Junior Bonner* died, with an obituary of losing money.

Steve, Sam, and violence were to move on with the success of *The Getaway*. Neither Steve or Sam were ever to make another quiet or—as some critics wrote, "gentle" or "elegiac"—film ever again.

Such a lack of commercial success moved me, for my next job, into the contemporary update of *Miracle on 34th Street* for CBS, and producer Norman Rosemont, with the gentle, dramatic brilliance of director Fielder Cook (like me, a graduate of Washington and Lee University).

Within eight years Steve would surrender his life to cancer, age fifty. Within twelve years, Sam would be gone, due to heart failure but no doubt it was the drugs, the alcohol, and all those years of hard living. He was fifty-eight when he passed.

There are evenings I watch *Wanted: Dead or Alive* (CBS, 1958-1961) on Starz Westerns Channel. There is the young McQueen building upon his reactions and the mannerisms to accompany them: the look, the smile, all which could be said without words. The ability to steal a scene, keeping the focus on him, as picking up an apple and chomping into it while the scene involves him watching two other actors with words. This scene-stealing escalated not too many years later when he reportedly drove Yul Brunner into fits of fury during *The Magnificent Seven*.

There are wonderful dramatic examples of this throughout *Junior Bonner*: the railroad depot scene, son and father, paying off in the wild cow-milking scene that followed, his moment in the Palace when he tells Ben Johnson how much he needed the rematch with Sunshine ("Money's nobody's favor, Buck"), and the family reunion, quietly reacting to a line I wrote that was one of his favorites: "Mom, do you have to smoke when you're feeding our baby?" It was a perfect line for Steve to react to, just the way it was perfected in *Wanted: Dead or Alive* years before.

Finally, in real life, at the end of filming, he stood in that bar in Jerome, when he did not have any money and I bought him a beer. I don't believe many writers began their relationship with Steve while on location with him throughout rehearsals and filming and ending up buying him a beer.

As for Sam—he turned out to be my great deceiver. He said nothing to me about hiding away in a Los Angeles hotel and rewriting my script. This was a habit he developed long before, rewriting *Gunsmoke* radio scripts for television. When he put his name on it and handed it to Marty Baum and Joe Wizan, they tossed his script. This resulted in him taking me on location where so often we worked well together, particularly after he learned I was the real deal cowboy, handling myself in the wild cow-milking and whenever he felt like putting me in the barrel.

Ever since that first day I met with producer Howard Christie on *The Virginian* in 1969 and he said, "Let's get a story," I have known television and film is a collaborative effort. I will never fail to admit the writing-for-character brilliance Sam added to my first draft. He had put himself through writing boot camp with the chance to rewrite *Gunsmoke* (CBS Radio,1952-1961) radio scripts, moving on to original teleplays and onto the big screen, when he burst into the film world with *Ride the High Country* (1962).

He demanded this same discipline from me. On our first trip to Prescott, we went through the entire script in the back of the car with Katy Haber taking notes. There was to be dinner with the mayor that night. I looked forward to it. It was not to be. "You're not going anywhere. You're goddam well going to start rewriting that script." Typewriter and paper were in my motel room. I rewrote that script for him in a week.

By the words of a screenplay I was being attached to a man who grew up with the love of home country in the shadow of the Sierra Nevada, with a violence to be witnessed with the Marines in 1945 China. He was raised by the strong-feared will of a mother he could never escape, and a father who was a man of the land, a home country so loved by Sam Peckinpah. He was more at ease with the moral code of Randolph Scott and Joel McCrea and those who would follow them on screen, than all the women who followed a failed marriage. He fell in the strongest within the bonds of male friendships with author Max Evans, actors Lee Marvin, Jason Robards, James Coburn, and select male comrades, adopting Kris Kristofferson, among others, on his journey toward the doom of drugs and alcohol. Perhaps in time he considered me for such an adoption. But I had Dorothy, and son Stuart and daughter Katherine. It was Sam who told young Stuart, "You hunt for meat, only to eat."

Max wrote *"Junior Bonner* was the best script Sam ever got his hands on."

Sam, Steve, and Jeb. We were all five years apart; Sam at forty-five, Steve at forty, and me turning thirty-five. We had different paths through life, and this added up to a trio who found empathy of family and the land in one original screenplay.

When Norman Jewison replaced Sam on *The Cincinnati Kid*, in 1964, he was quoted as telling Steve, "I can't be your father, Steve." Perhaps seven years later, Ace Bonner was the father figure who came for a visit.

A reviewer expressed disappointment in Sam for creating a hero who drove away and let his hometown be plowed under. But the reality of disappointment lay in Fresno County, California, where Sam's strong-willed mother, who burned forever in the depth of his soul, sold off her son's birthright land in favor of a housing development in the San Jouquin Valley. Leaving his land plowed under.

A journey returning to Yavapai County that began on February 14, 1958, with the passing of my mother, Jean Fallon Rosebrook at age fifty-four, and being drafted, with the Army not wanting me due to a history of asthma, leaving New York behind for advertising in Phoenix and Los Angeles, and a published novel, had found its way to a produced original screenplay. And for Dorothy, Stuart, and Katherine, money in a near-empty bank account.

As for my father, who I never saw more than three months a year after the age of nine, and even less after Dorothy and I married and moved to Los Angeles, he and I saw the film together in Charlottes-ville, Virginia. When my name came on the screen, in the darkness of the theater, he squeezed my arm.

He loved me. I loved him.

And that was better than a Hollywood ending.

During film production there is always time for fun and games on the set to lighten the atmosphere of the production schedule. Somewhere along the way, Sam Peckinpah acquired a tasseled umbrella (most likely leftover from the parade) to shade him and Katy Haber on the set. Mike Siegel Collection.

Prescott's iconic Yavapai County Courthouse Plaza across the street from the Palace was featured throughout Junior Bonner, *including in a key scene between Ben Johnson's rodeo stock contract character, Buck Roan, and Steve McQueen's Junior Bonner character.* Mike Siegel Collection.

The Reata Pass Steakhouse in Humboldt, Arizona, southeast of Prescott, was transformed into Curly Bonner's Outpost for selling Rio Ranchero mobile homes. Mike Siegel Collection.

Producer Joe Wizan was well-aware of the long-standing professional relationship between director of photography Lucien Ballard (left) and his camera crew and director Peckinpah, which gave him a great deal of confidence in green-lighting the production with less than a month to prepare to film Junior Bonner *at several locations in the Prescott, Arizona, area.* Mike Siegel Collection.

Ballard's camera crew worked seamlessly through the summer, at the numerous locations, including Reata Pass, with the electric and grip crews, led by gaffer Joseph Edesa and key grip Gaylin P. Schultz. Mike Siegel Collection.

Whatever the location, however Peckinpah wanted the shot set up, the camera,
grip, and electric crews were ready to adapt to the director's demands, including a
camera dolly set up on plywood to level the uneven ground at Reata Pass.
Mike Siegel Collection.

Idle time between scene set-ups at Elvira Bonner's house allowed time for the cast, crew, and family members—including from left to right: Jeb Rosebrook, (legs and feet visible), Sam Peckinpah, Ida Lupino, Robin Wizan, Steven Wizan, Katy Haber, and, Joe Wizan (back to camera)—to relax in the shade on a hot summer day in Prescott. Mike Siegel Collection.

The camera truck and Junior Bonner's Cadillac prepare to leave for principal photography on Highway 89 near Granite Dells, north of Prescott. Steve McQueen worked with the transportation captain James Thornsberry to season his Cadillac convertible to give it the road-weary look it carried, like a character unto itself, throughout the film. Mike Siegel Collection.

Veteran cinematographer Ballard in the white hat (making a call on the two-way phone) and his crew (including, it appears, Frank Kowalski up top in the middle) prepare for a day of principal photography filming the sequence of Junior Bonner *driving into Prescott.* Mike Siegel Collection.

Two of the key camera operators on Junior Bonner *were Chuck Arnold and Harry Young.* Mike Siegel Collection.

The camera and grip crew worked closely together to mount multiple cameras correctly for the driving shots of Steve McQueen in his Cadillac.
Mike Siegel Collection.

As a director, Peckinpah was known for his innovative and creative camera work, sometimes filming to excess later in his career, but his ability to get the coverage of the scenes with a creative camera, grip, and lighting crew, allowed him and his editing team the greatest creative latitude in the editing room.
Mike Siegel Collection.

In the last week of production, the camera crew and the Cadillac (note screenwriter Jeb Rosebrook in white jeans sitting in the middle on the running board) went out into Prescott Valley and to the Verde Valley near Jerome to film the final sequences of the movie. Photos Courtesy Mike Siegel Collection.

DOWN FOR SHOTS—The fiber glass horse over the entry of the Pioneer Store on Whiskey Row in Prescott was taken down last week and added to the cast of "Junior Bonner" movie after the quarantine of all live horses went into effect. The production department needed some footage of Steve McQueen driving his car and horse trailer around town. The "dummy" horse was painted the right color for the full-in role and hauled around with one cameraman in the car and another following the trailer for additional scenes of the tour.

The horse from above a Western wear store on Whiskey Row was borrowed to be a stunt double for McQueen's trailered horse in the final shooting sequences of Junior Bonner leaving and arriving into town, after Yavapai County declared an equine encephalitis emergency and the real movie horse was quarantined in Prescott.
Rosebrook Family Collection.

Peckinpah enjoyed having his family on set when he was on location, and he paid his daughter, Sharon Peckinpah, to be a dialogue coach on the film. She was also a patron in the Palace Bar scenes with her sisters Kristen and Melissa, while his son, Matthew Peckinpah, was cast as Tim Bonner, one of Curly's two sons.
Mike Siegel Collection.

The sequences filmed on U.S. Highway 89A of McQueen (a stand-in sits in the driver's seat while they set the shot) driving his Cadillac with the horse trailer during a thunderstorm rising over Mingus Mountain and Prescott Valley included McQueen raising the convertible roof as the rain began. The scene was the perfect ending of the movie, as another of the numerous serendipitous moments that summer of 1971. Mike Siegel Collection.

Katy Haber, Sam Peckinpah, and daughter Sharon Peckinpah enjoyed a moment while filming the last scenes of Junior Bonner *on U.S. Highway 89A, east of Prescott in August 1971.* Mike Siegel Collection.

Katy Haber and Steve McQueen became good friends on the set of Junior Bonner *and soon would be making another movie together when McQueen hired Peckinpah to direct their next picture,* The Getaway.
Mike Siegel Collection.

Lucien Ballard and Katy Haber shared a moment on the camera truck during the last days of principal photography in Prescott Valley. Mike Siegel Collection.

Scenes that did not make the final cut of the film were shot in the Verde Valley between Cottonwood and Clarkdale at the base of the old mining town of Jerome. After filming that day, the crew went up to Jerome for a meal, a few beers, and fun around the pool table. Mike Siegel Collection.

A magical moment the last day of filming has Lucien Ballard, Sam Peckinpah, Newt Arnold, and Katy Haber, in reflection near Jerome. Mike Siegel Collection.

Lucien Ballard and Sam Peckinpah's creative partnership as cinematographer and director dated back to 1959 and Peckinpah's short-lived TV series The Westerner. *Junior Bonner was their fifth collaboration. Ballard, who was sixty-seven in 1971 and had been in the movie business since 1929, hired on for one more Peckinpah-McQueen film after* Junior Bonner *as cinematographer for* The Getaway *(1972), the next film for all three of them, as well as the third film Ballard made with the iconic Hollywood star.* Mike Siegel Collection.

EPILOGUE: A CURTAIN CALL

STEVE McQUEEN

The memory is always with me: "Why am I called Junior?" Cutting lines, too much to say, and I was "Shakespeare." Coming to your home with Joe. The first question you ever asked of me: "Doesn't he take notes?" How much you loved your kids—selling their tie-dyed tee shirts. You and Barbara, "Why do they call you Junior?" "I don't know." I wrote to you in your last days in Mexico and signed it "Shakespeare."

In all our time together, from that evening we met at your home, I never invaded your space and you never invaded mine. Meeting Dorothy and smiling down on Katherine, I think you realized I was a father, as you were. We never had a disagreement over my words, except over apple pie with Ida. We started *Junior* together and we ended it together. And it was good.

SAM PECKINPAH

Your memorial. The many clips from our film, the "Master of Violence" saluting you. Months before you left us, your call wanting me to write with you on *The Last Running* and an old buffalo named Shakespeare. I am haunted by what could have been from that novel and us.

Your fiftieth birthday party. Dorothy and I brought you a bottle of bourbon with a top statuette of Rocky Marciano. You wrote to Dorothy, "Thank you for Rocky. But why did you have to bring Jeb? Love, Sam." We were both the "Worst Pool Players in North America." And you never tied a tin can to my ass and mailed me home. In fact, I would learn years later that you went off to a hotel room before Prescott and rewrote my screenplay and put your name on it with mine. Mary Baum and Joe tossed it out. Strike three.

JOE WIZAN

You in your office at Warner's preparing to head for Utah to produce your first film to be called *Jeremiah Johnson*. Mike Wise had sent me to you because Jim Coburn had not yet made *Ward Craft* and I was near broke and Robert Redford had not responded to my *Bonner* outline. Joe optioned *Bonner* with enough money for me to write the screenplay. Joe said, "I want this for Steve McQueen." We were the same age. Years later, he brought me back into his life to polish, rewrite *Fire in the Sky* (1993). Lunches where I was included with his California Air National Guard buddies: Joe Byrne, Johnny Wilder, David Nelson. He never went east of Santa Monica to keep himself in fresh air or lose his tan. He once told me how he challenged himself to sleep with a woman without sex, to show he cared for her. He bought one of his wives a horse and named him Junior. Dementia took my friend Joe. And damn, that hurt.

BEN JOHNSON

As Steve predicted, Ben won an Academy Award as Best Supporting Actor for his performance in *The Last Picture Show* (1971). I have so many memories of the man who once told Dorothy and me the barn and horse corral (and the horse in it) and the land on it made him more money than all three hundred films he appeared in. "Those folks coming off the plane, with a suitcase full of cash and the red dot on their forehead." A one-time world champion team roper, I never saw a man, either in person, or in the movies, who could ride a horse like Ben Johnson. At Nudie's Western Store in North Hollywood, Ben offered Dorothy and me a deal on a Montana acre lot, $125 and no interest. We never built, the development never took off to Ben's or our expectations. But what the hell, Ben was a friend. He was real.

ROBERT PRESTON

I heard second (or third or fourth) hand that Bob considered the part of Ace Bonner right up there among the best characters he ever played. Oh, the rhythm of his dialogue! I only wish I had the opportunity to write for him again. There was never a scene or dialogue he wanted changed. From where on my dad's 1948 Royal typewriter came the gift of such words?—"Up to the mouth and over the gums, look out stomach, here it comes." "If this world is all about winners, what's for the losers?" Lung cancer took Bob.

IDA LUPINO

Marty Baum never hesitated. Susan Hayward was on the plane back to Florida. Ida was his choice. Like Patricia Neal brought strength from Paul Newman in *Hud*, Ida brought it out in Steve, especially when she promised him he would be eating a lot of apple pie if he did not come back the next day knowing the lines as written. But her finest moment was on the back stairs of the Palace with Bob, who wanted her to go to Australia with him; so dramatically strong, Sam actually considered filming a scene with them on the plane together heading for the land Down Under. She loved telling the story of escaping Darryl Zanuck clutching her legs on his knees in his office. Just before leaving Prescott, Ida learned her husband, Howard Duff, had left her for a younger woman. Although she would continue to act in film and television until 1978, her life was never the same. Cancer and a stroke took her in 1995.

MARY MURPHY

I fell in love with Mary watching her in her first film with Marlon Brando in *The Wild One* (1953). So it was an unexpected, welcomed surprise for me when Sam cast her as Ruth, Joe Don Baker's wife. Sam had his reasons. As his writing career in television took off, he somehow got between "Wells Fargo's" Dale Robertson and Mary. One day at Sam's rented home in Prescott she looked at me and said, "smile." It was early on in the filming and she recognized my initial homesickness for my family. At the age of eighty, in 2011, Mary passed on of heart disease. I will always regret I never got to see her again. And her very special line: "Mom, do you have to smoke when you're feeding our baby?"

CASEY TIBBS

He was, as he described himself, "Possibly America's Most Beloved Cowboy." I had remembered Casey on the cover of *Life* magazine. After filming, he agreed to work with me on a biography on his life. Sadly, the offers were very low because Casey would not do as Jim Bouton had done in *Ball Four* with tell-all tales of sex, involving him and his rodeo contemporaries. Casey became a virtual member of our family, teaching Stuart and Katherine to ride, emotionally embracing our friend Merle Frost's mentally challenged son, Tad. He had a small French-made convertible (he lived with Renee, his French beauty) and there were Saturdays when he would bring Stuart and Katherine along on our travels and Katherine would always ask, "Where are we going, Casey?" He would answer, "I'll tell you when we get there." *Floating Horses* (2017), a documentary on Casey's life, has recently been completed. Cancer took our friend too soon at age sixty-one. No "possibly" with Casey, he *was* our most beloved cowboy.

BILL McKINNEY

Until his major breakthrough in *Deliverance*, Bill was taking the roles he could and surviving as a teacher and arborist. Not long after filming, Dorothy and I invited Bill and his then lady friend out to trim the two lemon trees in our backyard. He gave them such a buzz cut, they died! Against Dorothy's warnings, he and I managed to cut a limb off a guava tree that held a hummingbird nest with two eggs. "I pouted for two days," she remembers. We tried to reattach the nest, but it did not work. However, we still have the preserved nest. Bill had a long run in Clint Eastwood films, most notably in *The Outlaw Josey Wales* (1976). He guest-appeared in *The Yellow Rose* (NBC, 1983-1984) television series for which I worked as a writer-producer. The last time I saw Bill was on the street in Toluca Lake in Los Angeles telling me in the Tennessee accent that never left him, even through The Actor's Studio in New York, a tale of his recent show business fatherhood. Bill was gone at eighty. Unforgettable!

DUB TAYLOR

One of young son Stuart's most memorable moments during that summer filming was riding with then-sixty-four-year-old Dub in a Landrover. An accomplished and modest actor, who began with Frank Capra, then playing the sidekick character of "Cannonball" with a host of B-movie cowboy heroes, he was, by *Junior Bonner*, a member of Sam's stock company. I loved being around Dub. He was all humor and wit and talent with nothing more to prove than who he was. A talented football player at Alabama who grew up in Virginia and Georgia, he left the 1938 Rose Bowl team, like star Johnny Mack Brown, to pursue Hollywood. Dub left us, age eighty-seven, after a heart attack.

DON "RED" BARRY

Don "Red" as we called him, made sure the rodeo announcer let the public know he was among the top motion picture draws of 1944 or one of the wartime years. Becoming well known as a Republic B-movie star in the role of Red Ryder, Don "Red," a five-foot-four bandy rooster former college football player from Texas, had a long career in film and television with credits from 1938 to 1981. Stuart and I ran into him at the North Hollywood Library not too long after Prescott. Sadly, Don "Red" at the age of sixty-eight, in an altercation with his wife in 1980, shot and killed himself as the police arrived. There were, among us kids who followed cowboy movies, those who believed Don Red was the best. (Charles Starrett, the "Durango Kid," was mine.)

MACK HARDING

My close friend, writer/producer John Wilder describes Mack Harding as "one of the best men I have ever known. Absolutely honest, smart as a whip, as authentic as a man can be."

Mack arrived as an assistant director in the wake of Sam's firings. Sam was fortunate to have Mack, treated him with the respect he deserved and did not trifle with him. Later, Mack was an important part of John Wilder's adaptation of the mini-series of James Michener's *Centennial* (NBC, 1978-1979. "Every film I produced after that, I always went to Mack first," Wilder told me years later. "But by that time a lot of people had learned how good he was at his work, and timing never permitted our working together again. We remained tight friends, though, and I often sought his counsel in weighing production decisions. He left us too soon." I drove home from Prescott with Mack.

As a newly born writer with his first film credit, I knew I was riding with class.

TED HAWORTH

Like all the others I was privileged to work with, Ted was a most talented man of greatness as an art director/production designer. Joe Wizan had brought him on board following *Jeremiah Johnson* on which Ted had worked with director Sidney Pollack and Robert Redford. I learned daily what his creative eye added to the film. Since nearly all the locations were already in place, Ted put important added touches to them, especially Curly Bonner's Trading Post. Ted told others he compared my writing to one of my idols, Paddy Chayefsky, as Ted's initial professional work was seen in Alfred Hitchcock's classic *Strangers on a Train* (1951) and in *Marty* (1955). He never spoke to me about his Academy Award for *Sayonara* (1957) or his later work on *Some Like It Hot* (1959) or *The Longest Day* (1962). Ted left us at age seventy-seven, the result of an auto accident in Sundance, Utah.

SANDRA DEEL

Chosen by Marty Baum to play Ace Bonner's love interest, Nurse Arlis, Sandra came to the film from Broadway as a singer/actress. While her career was not as well-known as many others' in the cast, Sandra fit in quickly and comfortably. Sandra was a terrific person to know, lots of fun with a great, outgoing personality. Sometime after completion of the filming, she played the lead in a Los Angeles musical production of *No, No, Nannette* and Dorothy took Katherine to see her and visit backstage. Sandra left us at age eighty.

FRANK KOWALSKI

I've seldom met anyone to match the wit, humor, and creative savvy of Frank Kowalski. Frank could do anything on a film from dialogue director to second unit directing to writing. His close friendship with Sam would sadly end on *Junior Bonner*, even as Frank and Sam were working on Frank's story that would become *Bring Me the Head of Alfredo Garcia*. His brother Bernie was an outstanding director, his father a film editor under Michael Curtiz, but Frank and Emma Kowalski are the couple the Rosebrooks will always remember. Frank was loved and respected by so many. Take a bow for us all, Frank as, in your words, "Top Hat and Tails!" Parkinson's took Frank far too early.

MARTIN BAUM

How quickly my life changed after Joe and I had our initial visit with Steve. Then it was off to meet Joe's mentor from CMA and now president of ABC Pictures, Marty Baum, then forty-seven years old. From there it would be my initial meeting with Sam, from there to Steve meeting two young actresses in Marty's offices with me writing dance dialogue for them ("How about some honey from my hive?" or something akin) and from there to the disaster with Susan Hayward to meeting and casting Bob Preston and Ida Lupino. From there to my first meeting in his office with Sam Peckinpah. A veteran of the Normandy Invasion, Marty, his talent agency time in New York moves to L.A. in 1961. Marty Baum was always appreciative of my screenplay and never wavered his support in me via Joe. In his later career with Creative Artists, he was given all the respect this man was due. He left us at age seventy-six.

JAMES COBURN

In the fall of 1971, Dorothy and I stood with Jim in the darkness outside his Tower Road home in Beverly Hills. We were leaving the pre-filming party for *Ward Craft*. Lots of joints and Jack Daniels available. Actor James Barrymore, then living with the Coburns, had painted an abstract portrait of his vision of Ward. Sadly, Nixon froze prices due to the Vietnam War expense and the

Japanese backers dropped out. He died of a heart attack in 2002 while listening to classical music with his beautiful wife, Paula. He was seventy-four.

MIKE WISE

When Mike had put my writing together with Coburn, it led to the open door with Joe Wizan and Steve, CMA clients. Because of Mike, I was accepted. Our strong relationship continued until CMA was sold into International Creative Artists and he was not included. I went to newly formed CAA. Mike and I reunited with several more agencies and his production career until the last year of his life, in 2016.

ROSS DOLLARHIDE, JR.

World champion steer wrestler, 1953. A premier stuntman for many years, Ross died of internal injuries from a horse fall while filming the television series *The Oregon Trail* (NBC, 1976–1977) in 1977. He was fifty-six years old.

JIMMY SHEPPARD

Jimmy was part of the dangerous bridge explosion in *The Wild Bunch* and joined the bar fight in the Palace. Jimmy died from being dragged by a horse during the filming of *Comes a Horseman* while doubling Jason Robards. Jimmy was forty years old.

NORMAN "BILL" FAIN II

For years, on the dirt roads from Orme leading to Prescott, we passed the family home of the Fain Ranch at Dewey. Since 1874 the Fain family has ranched in central Arizona. As miners and ranchers took the land from the Apaches, so Bill Fain turned ranch land into pioneering the Town of Prescott Valley. Bill Fain was in the infancy of his creation on that July day in 1970, as I rode the highway with R. Kirk Dunbar. It was enough to inspire the story concept of *Junior Bonner*. Today the Town of Prescott Valley that

Bill Fain pioneered has over 38,000 or so citizens. Bill passed away in August of 2016 at the age of seventy-eight.

In a way we two grew up neighbors but never met. I am sorry we did not.

AND A FINAL BOW TO JERRY FIELDING

Dorothy and I sat with Jerry and his wife, Camille, in their Hollywood Hills home listening to the score to *Junior Bonner*. No greater honor could come to me than to hear a score composed by the genius of a man who had brought the brilliant music to Sam's *The Wild Bunch*. As we left that evening, I told Jerry I was so emotionally moved by his score, I believed I could have written the screenplay to his music for the film. Dorothy and I were in the company of a giant of the history of big band and film-composing history. As I sit writing this in a small office in Scottsdale, Arizona, I am truly humbled by my good fortune in writing for those whose talent visited my words and story filmed in Prescott.

We sat near Jerry at Sam's fiftieth birthday in 1976. Jerry remarked he had brought his doctor with him in case his heart should begin to go. Four years later, at age fifty-seven, Jerry was gone.

Jerry once told an interviewer, "I'm not corruptible at all. I'm not for sale." It was the honest code of a man never less than true to his word and his talent.

DAVID MacKECHNIE

My friend and neighbor in North Hollywood/Van Nuys, David and his wife, Marie, became lifelong friends following our introduction by Jerry Fielding. While his song "Seven Rings of Silver" was not included in the soundtrack of *Junior Bonner*, MacKechnie was part of Fielding's musical team that assisted him during the scoring of the film. David was part of the great songwriting generation that came out of Nashville in the late 1960s, and many of his songs were recorded by top artists, including John Denver ("Sweet Melinda"), Kenny Rogers ("The Farther You Go, the Closer I Get"), and Martina McBride (#11, "Phones are Ringin' All Over Town"). In addition to his songwriting talent, he was a great athlete, and we regularly played racquetball with our neighbors and friends, Gaynor Peet and Bruce Brinkema. He was a member of the Irish and International Songwriters Guild. He passed away on October 1, 2017. He will be greatly missed.

YES AND YOU, TOO BOBBY VISIGLIA, the wiliest, craftiest, most talented prop man and Liar's Poker player perhaps in the history of motion pictures!

AND TO ALL WHO REMAIN WITH US: Bill Pierce, Katy Haber, Lynn Stalmaster, Chalo Gonzalez, Barbara Leigh, Mickey Gilbert, Floyd Baze, Frank Kelly, Joe Don Baker, Rod Hart, Frank Baur, and all who were in wardrobe, hair, makeup, wranglers, Teamsters, and extras, and Frank Bauer, who I could not locate, I thank you.

The End

ABC Pictures held the Los Angeles premier of Junior Bonner *at Grauman's Chinese Theatre in Hollywood in June 1972.* Rosebrook Family Collection.

ABC Pictures promoted Junior Bonner *globally, producing books and international posters to accompany the film at premieres around the world, including this Japanese premiere booklet from 1972.*

Rosebrook Family Collection.

My lifelong friend from high school, R. Kirk "Sandy" Dunbar, who had convinced me to go to Prescott for the Fourth of July in 1970, visited Dorothy and me in North Hollywood after the release of Junior Bonner *to celebrate and remember that fateful life-changing trip to the Prescott rodeo.* Rosebrook Family Collection.

When my wife, Dorothy, and our daughter, Katherine, came to Prescott for a week after the Fourth of July, they bought an Indian-style turquoise dress that Katherine wore almost every day afterwards, including for an afternoon at the park. Photo by Dorothy Rosebrook, Rosebrook Family Collection.

After Jeb Rosebrook was on location for most of the summer of 1971, he was grateful to be at home the following summer with Dorothy in North Hollywood. They were grateful for Junior Bonner *and how it changed his career and their family's financial stability.*
Photo by Stuart Rosebrook, Rosebrook Family Collection.

My father John "Jack" Rosebrook was a highly lauded advertising copy writer for Young & Rubicam in New York City, and he viewed my decision to leave my advertising job as financially foolish. We enjoyed a good reunion after Junior Bonner *was released, and a renewal of our relationship before his passing in 1977.*

Photo by Don Dornan, Rosebrook Family Collection.

After my son, Stuart, finished his two weeks at the Orme School's Quarter Circle
V Bar Ranch Camp, he came and stayed with us at the Prescottonian Hotel,
where one morning he got a surprise from actor Dub Taylor: a four-wheel-drive
adventure into the hills around Prescott.

Photo by Dorothy Rosebrook, Rosebrook Family Collection.

For many years following the production of Junior Bonner, *Casey Tibbs was a regular guest at the Rosebrook family home and dinner table in North Hollywood, entertaining our children, Stuart and Katherine, with stories of horses and rodeos, and even taking them out for riding lessons to a friend's ranch in Newhall, California.* Rosebrook Family Collection.

After Junior Bonner *wrapped production and was released, our family friendship with Casey Tibbs and Ben Johnson grew over the years, and included a reunion at an old-timers rodeo in Tehachapi, California.*
Rosebrook Family Collection.

In Italy, where Westerns, Sam Peckinpah, and Steve McQueen have never lost their popularity, Junior Bonner *was* L'Ultimo Buscadero.
Mike Siegel Collection.

In Japan, Steve McQueen was the featured star in marketing Junior Bonner.
Mike Siegel Collection.

Steve McQueen's box office fame extended across Latin America, including Junior Bonner's *distribution to Argentina.* Mike Siegel Collection.

Cinema is very popular in Belgium, and the pairing of Sam Peckinpah and Steve McQueen in Junior Bonner *helped make the film profit internationally.*
Mike Siegel Collection.

Sam Peckinpah and Steve McQueen were popular with cinema fans in Germany when Junior Bonner *was released in 1972, and its success at the box office helped the film's international bottom line—and the overall profit of the film.* Mike Siegel Collection.

Junior Bonner *grossed more internationally ($2.9 million) than domestically ($1.9 million), including distribution in Finland.* Mike Siegel Collection.

The pairing of maverick director Peckinpah and the box-office star McQueen with an all-star supporting cast, including film noir legend Ida Lupino, made Junior Bonner *a critical success in France.* Mike Siegel Collection.

When Junior Bonner *was distributed in Mexico in 1972, movie fans there were already familiar with Peckinpah, who had filmed* The Wild Bunch *in Mexico, and with McQueen, an international box-office star.* Mike Siegel Collection.

ABC pictures produced two primary one-sheet posters for the promotion of Junior Bonner, *one an illustrative design marketing the picture as a rodeo movie, with McQueen walking with his rodeo saddle, and the less familiar one-sheet collage that attempted to broaden the appeal of the picture to a wider audience than rodeo fans.* Both Posters Mike Siegel Collection.

For a decade British cinema fans had faithfully supported the careers of Sam Peckinpah and Steve McQueen, and as a follow-up to the ultra-violent Straw Dogs, *filmed in the United Kingdom the year before,* Junior Bonner *was a welcome surprise for British movie-goers. As London's* Guardian *newspaper film critic Michael McNay wrote about* Junior Bonner *on July 20, 1972, "ANOTHER Peckinpah, another elegiac Western: but this one wears its rue with a difference. And it's the best of the bunch."* Mike Siegel Collection.

ABC Pictures was able to distribute Junior Bonner *even behind the Iron Curtain, to Marshall Tito's Yugoslavia.* Mike Siegel Collection.

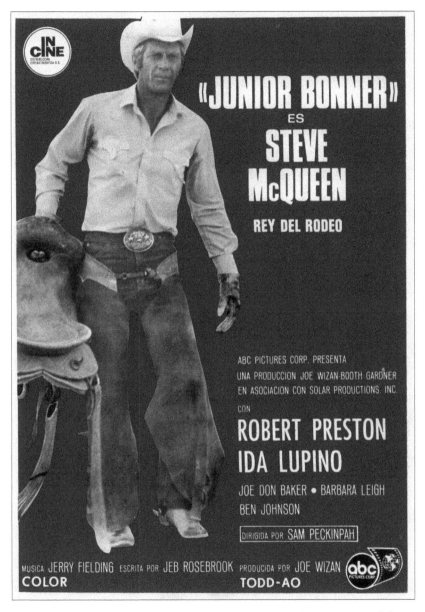

Spanish film-goers, who enjoyed a Western cinema tradition, welcomed the release of Junior Bonner. Mike Siegel Collection.

SLOVENSKÁ
POŽIČOVŇA FILMOV
BRATISLAVA **Junior Bonner** FILM USA

ABC Pictures was able to distribute Junior Bonner *into communist-controlled Czechoslovakia, where Steve McQueen's role as an aging cowboy hero was a surprise hit.* Mike Siegel Collection.

Junior Bonner *was distributed nationally in Canada and enjoyed great publicity across the country, including the cover of* Key to Toronto *in September 1972.*
Rosebrook Family Collection.

Twenty-five years after the summer of 1971, Junior Bonner *was the cover story of the centennial anniversary program of the Prescott Frontier Days Rodeo in July 1996.* Rosebrook Family Collection.

*After riding in the parade as honorary grand marshal, Jeb and son Stuart Rosebrook
(left) stopped to have a beer at the Palace Saloon, but because of a real estate dispute,
for the first time in anyone's memory, the Palace on Whiskey Row was chained
shut on the Fourth of July. Later that year, new owner Dave Michelson bought the
Palace, and with a great deal of investment in restoring it and updating the historic
building, reopened it as the Palace Restaurant and Saloon.*
Rosebrook Family Collection.

Jeb and Dorothy Rosebrook enjoyed returning to Prescott twenty-five years after the summer of 1971, when Jeb was honored by the Prescott Frontier Days Rodeo Committee as honorary grand marshal. Rosebrook Family Collection.

Since first meeting on the production set of Junior Bonner *in Prescott in the summer of 1971, Barbara Leigh and Katy Haber have remained good friends.* Courtesy Barbara Leigh.

Since Junior Bonner *was released in 1972, the film has become an international fan favorite and been consistently considered one of Steve McQueen, Sam Peckinpah, and Jeb Rosebrook's best films. In 2001, Steve McQueen as Junior Bonner graced the cover of* Arizona Highways.
Rosebrook Family Collection.

On special assignment for The Arizona Republic, *Arizona historian, artist, and executive editor of* True West *magazine Bob Boze Bell interpreted Steve McQueen's role as Junior Bonner for a pre-Fourth of July edition of the paper.*
Courtesy Rosebrook Family Collection.

In 2016, Prescott's Frontier Days Rodeo invited Jeb Rosebrook to serve as the parade's honorary grand marshal on the forty-fifth anniversary of the filming of Junior Bonner *in 1971. He and Dorothy awaited the beginning of the parade at Murphy's Restaurant.*

In 2016, Jeb and Dorothy Rosebrook rode in the Prescott Frontier Days Parade, forty-five years after Peckinpah and the Junior Bonner *film company filmed the actual parade in real time with the production's addition of Curly Bonner's float and Preston and McQueen's wild ride.*
Photos by Stuart Rosebrook, Rosebrook Family Collection.

Forty-five years after production started, screenwriter Jeb Rosebrook pointed to his name on the Palace Saloon mural dedicated to Junior Bonner *and the making of the film in the Palace and Prescott.*

Seventy-one years after he came to Arizona from Connecticut for the first time at nine years old to study and board at the Orme School because of his asthma, screenwriter Jeb Rosebrook enjoyed returning to his adopted hometown of Prescott as honorary grand marshal of the Prescott Frontier Days Rodeo in 2016.

Photos by Stuart Rosebrook, Rosebrook Family Collection.

On October 31, 2017, Disney and distributor Kino Lorber re-released Junior Bonner *on DVD and the brand-new Blu-Ray edition, both with six new special features produced by Mike Siegel, including* Passion & Poetry: Rodeo Time, *a fifty-four-minute film that features Jeb Rosebrook;* Junior Bonner Remembered *produced by Keith Woods; and audio commentary by Sam Peckinpah biographers Paul Seydor, Garner Simmons, and David Weddle, moderated by film historian Nick Redman.* Rosebrook Family Collection.

Mastered in HD - Screen icon Steve McQueen (*Love with the Proper Stranger, Bullitt*) is at his rugged best in this totally captivating tale of a fading rodeo champion from acclaimed director Sam Peckinpah (*The Getaway, Bring Me the Head of Alfredo Garcia, Convoy*). With his bronco-busting career on its last legs, Junior Bonner (McQueen) heads to his hometown to try his luck in the annual rodeo. But his fond childhood memories are shattered when he finds his family torn apart by his greedy brother (Joe Don Baker, *Framed*) and hard-drinking father (Robert Preston, *The Music Man*). Now Junior must break the wildest bull in the West to bring his family together for one final moment of cowboy glory in the roughest, rowdiest ride of his life! *Junior Bonner* is an extraordinarily graceful yet unflinching rendering of a slice of Americana, beautifully shot by the great Lucien Ballard (*The Ballad of Cable Hogue*) and featuring a top-notch cast which also includes Ida Lupino (*Road House*), Ben Johnson (*The Wild Bunch*), Mary Murphy (*Beachhead*), Dub Taylor (*Burnt Offerings*), Don 'Red' Barry (*Shalako*) and Bill McKinney (*Deliverance*).

SPECIAL FEATURES:

- PASSION & POETRY – RODEO TIME 56 Min
- PASSION & POETRY – PECKINPAH ANECDOTES 26 Min
- AUDIO COMMENTARY by Sam Peckinpah Authors Paul Seydor, Garner Simmons and David Weddle, moderated by Film Historian Nick Redman
- JB TRIVIA 5 Min • JB REMEMBERED 3 Min • THREE JB Animated Image Galleries
- US Theatrical Trailer • TWO US Radio Spots • US TV Spot

ABC PICTURES CORPORATION IN ASSOCIATION WITH WIZAN PRODUCTIONS & SOLAR PRODUCTIONS, INC. PRESENT A SAM PECKINPAH FILM "JUNIOR BONNER" STEVE McQUEEN ROBERT PRESTON IDA LUPINO BEN JOHNSON JOE DON BAKER PRODUCED JOE WIZAN MUSIC MICKEY BOROFSKY SCREENPLAY JEB ROSEBROOK MUSIC JERRY FIELDING DIRECTED SAM PECKINPAH

PG

1972 Color 100 Minutes Anamorphic (2.35:1) Subtitles: English

KINO LORBER   DVD   THIS DISC IS COPY PROTECTED   □□ DOLBY. DIGITAL

7 38329 21651 1

BIBLIOGRAPHY

Books

Antoniades, Andrew and Siegel, Mike. *Steve McQueen: The Actor and His Films.* Deerfield, Ill.: Dalton Watson Fine Books, 2011.

Donati, William. *Ida Lupino: A Biography.* Lexington, Ky.: University Press of Kentucky, 1996.

Evans, Max, as told to Robert Nott. *Goin' Crazy with Sam Peckinpah and All Our Friends.* Albuquerque, N.M.: University of New Mexico Press, 2014.

Evans, Max. *Sam Peckinpah: Master of Violence—Being the Account of the Making of a Movie, and Other Sundry Things.* Vermillion, S.D.: Dakota Press, 1972.

Fine, Marshall. *Bloody Sam: The Life and Films of Sam Peckinpah.* New York, NY: Donald I. Fine, Inc., 1991.

Gilbert, Mickey with Rebecca Rockell. *Me and My Saddle Pal: My Life as a Hollywood Stunt Man.* Denver, Co.: Outskirts Press, 2014.

Jones, J.R. *The Lives of Robert Ryan.* Middleton, Conn.: Wesleyan University Press, 2015

Leigh, Barbara with Marshall Terrill. *The King, McQueen and The Love Machine: My Secret Hollywood Life with Elvis Presley, Steve McQueen and James Aubrey.* Bloomington, Ind.: XLibris Corp., 2001.

McKinney, Doug. *Sam Peckinpah.* Boston: Twayne Publishers, 1979.

Sayer, John W. *The Santa Fe, Prescott & Phoenix Railway: The Scenic Line of Arizona.* Boulder, Col.: Pruett, 1990.

Seydor, Paul. *The Authentic Death & Contentious Afterlife of Pat Garrett and Billy the Kid: The Untold Story of Peckinpah's Last Western Film.* Evanston, Ill.: Northwestern University Press, 2015.

-------. Peckinpah: *The Western Films—A Reconsideration.* Urbana and Chicago, Ill.: University of Illinois Press, 1980, 1997.

Simmons, Garner. *Peckinpah: A Portrait in Montage.* Austin, Texas: University of Texas Press, 1976.

------------. *Peckinpah: A Portrait in Montage: With a New Preface and Postscript.* New York, N.Y.: Limelight Editions, 1998.

Terrill, Marshall. *Steve McQueen: The Life and Legend of a Hollywood Icon.* Chicago, Ill.: Triumph Books, 2010.

--------. *Steve McQueen: A Tribute to the King of Cool.* Deerfield, Ill., Dalton Watson Fine Books, 2010.

Weddle, David. "If They Move…Kill 'Em!": The Life and Times of Sam Peckinpah. New York, N.Y.: Grove Press 1994.

Archives

Jerry Fielding Papers, L. Tom Perry Special Collections; BYU Film Music
   Archives; 1130 Harold B. Lee Library; Brigham Young University; Provo,
   Utah 84602; http://sc.lib.byu.edu/
Junior Bonner Correspondence, 1971, 1-f.7, Steve McQueen Papers, Production Papers-Produced, *Junior Bonner;* Margaret Herrick Library, Academy
   of Motion Pictures, Arts & Sciences, Beverly Hills, California 90211; www.
   collections.org

Internet

WWW.IBDB.com
WWW.IMDB.com
WWW.REPETOIRE.BMI.COM

ABOUT THE AUTHORS

JEB ROSEBROOK

Born in New York City, New York, in 1935, Jeb Rosebrook has earned his living as a professional writer since he first was a paid intern as a dramatic television writer at NBC in 1956 in New York. His career includes journalism, advertising, public relations, three published novels, and over thirty years of credits in film and television, including one Emmy nomination as co-writer of *I Will Fight No More Forever: the Story of Chief Joseph* and two Writers Guild of America nominations for best television dramas, the two-hour *The Waltons'* episode "The Conflict," and his adaptation of the novel, *The Prince of Central Park*. Film credits include the Sam Peckinpah-directed classic, *Junior Bonner*, starring Steve McQueen, and Disney's iconic sci-fi classic *The Black Hole* (1977). Television credits for writing and co-writing and producing include numerous television films and mini-series, including Kenny Rogers' *The Gambler*, *The Yellow Rose*, and *The Outsiders*. He also adapted "The Conflict" with Earl Hamner, into a stage play, available through Dramatic Publishing, with permission of Earl Hamner and Warner Brothers.

Currently, he is writing the third of his American Trilogy, the first two being *Purgatory Road: The Road Between Heaven and Hell* set in 1951 Arizona and introducing Charlemagne, a deadly Mojave rattlesnake, and *Forever More: Only the Beginning*, when Charlemagne visits 1954 Virginia and meets God, desegregation and rock 'n' roll.

Jeb is a graduate of The Orme School, Mayer, Arizona, and Washington & Lee University, Lexington, Virginia. He and his wife of fifty-seven years, Dorothy, live in Scottsdale, Arizona.

STUART ROSEBROOK, PH.D.

Born in Santa Monica, California, Stuart Rosebrook is a professional historian, editor, and writer. He has over thirty years of professional experience in the media industry, including television production, television news, magazine and book publishing, nonprofits, editorial services to publications, creative and production services for television and film companies, and branding, advertising, public relations, marketing, and communications strategies for corporate and nonprofit clients. He is currently the senior editor for *True West* magazine of Cave Creek, Arizona, while working on numerous freelance writing and editing projects, including writing the history of ABC Television's 1969-1971 series, *The Johnny Cash Show.*

He is the author of *At Work in Arizona: the First 100 Years*, with curator Marilyn Szabo, for Alliance Bank of Arizona (2014), and, with Bob Boze Bell and the editorial team of *True West, The True West Ultimate Travel Guide* (2017).

He is married to Julie E. Rosebrook, Ph.D., a psychologist at the Coralville V.A. and father of two children, Jeb and Kristina. They live in Iowa City, Iowa.

CPSIA information can be obtained
at www.ICGtesting.com
Printed in the USA
LVHW061932160723
752503LV00005B/225